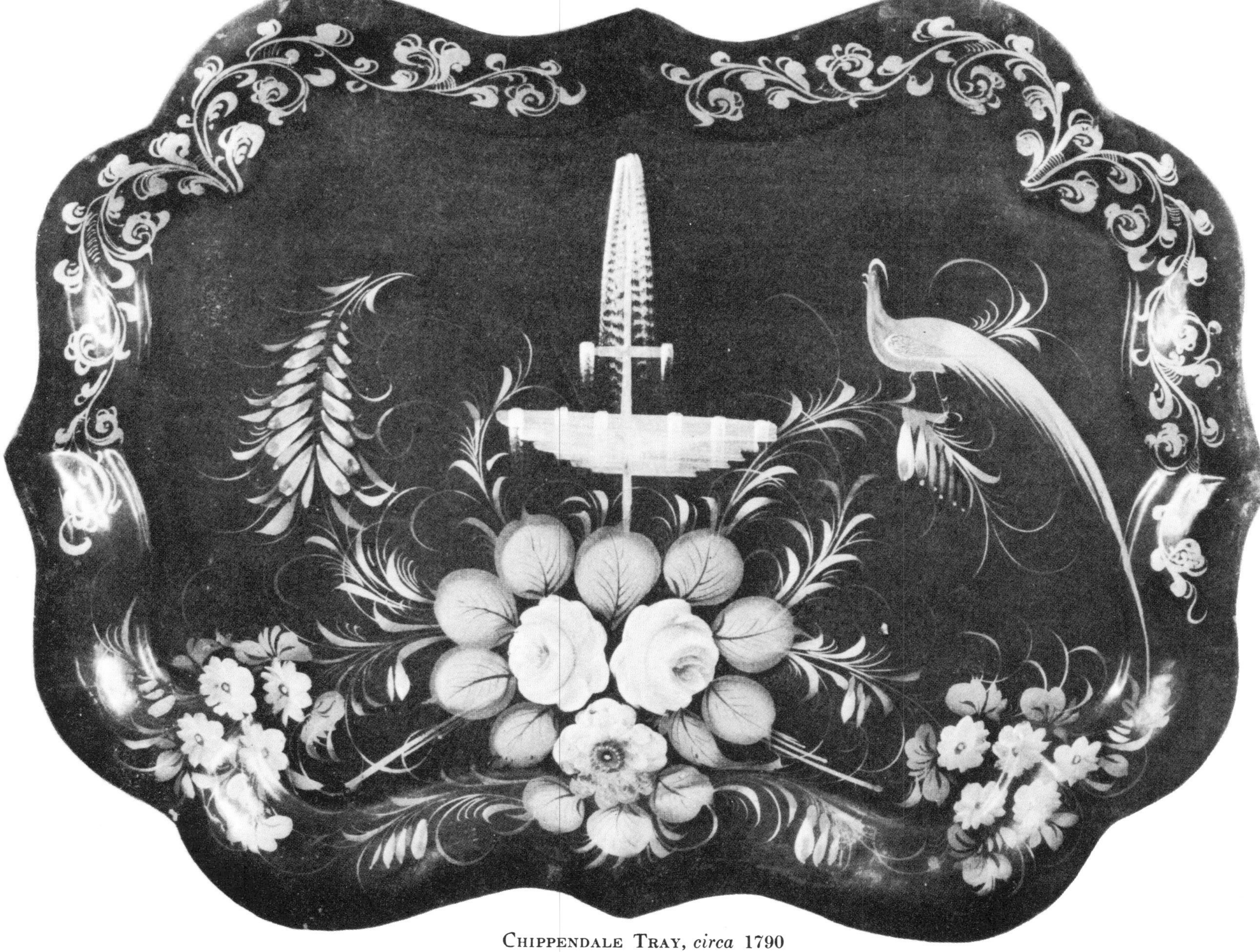

Chippendale Tray, *circa* 1790

TRADITIONAL TOLE PAINTING

WITH AUTHENTIC ANTIQUE DESIGNS AND WORKING DIAGRAMS FOR STENCILING AND BRUSH-STROKE PAINTING

Adaptable for Trays, Boxes, Chests, Chairs and Other Furniture

Roberta Ray Blanchard

DOVER PUBLICATIONS, INC.
NEW YORK

Published in Canada by General Publishing Company, Ltd., 30 Lesmill Road, Don Mills, Toronto,
Ontario.
Published in the United Kingdom by Constable
and Company, Ltd.

This Dover edition, first published in 1977, is
an unabridged and corrected republication of the
work first published by the Charles T. Branford
Company, Boston, in 1949 under the title *How to
Paint Trays*.

International Standard Book Number: 0-486-23531-9
Library of Congress Catalog Card Number: 77-78208

Manufactured in the United States of America
Dover Publications, Inc.
180 Varick Street
New York, N. Y. 10014

FOREWORD

The Author wishes to acknowledge the kindness and cooperation of the following organizations in the compiling of this book:

The Society for the Preservation of New England Antiquities.

The Metropolitan Museum of Art, Print Department.

The Philadelphia Museum of Art.

Thanks are also due many individuals and friends who have permitted treasured heirlooms to be photographed for the book. Particular thanks are due Harold H. Blanchard, without whose advice and cooperation the work could not have been completed.

ROBERTA RAY BLANCHARD

Winchester, Massachusetts

CONTENTS

INTRODUCTION

Have you ever looked at a nice wooden box too pretty to throw away, or a tired tin tray too battered to use, and said: "Some day I will do something with that — maybe even decorate it"? Then, because you are not certain of the kind of paints to use or the type of brushes needed, "some day" never seems to come.

Perhaps you even feel that you are not "artistic," and tray-painting or putting posies on knobs of the old dresser is all right for your next-door neighbor, but not for you. This book then is written for the purpose of telling you that anyone who has hands can paint, and that painting is fun! Indeed, if once you start this engaging occupation the chances are that you will become such a devotee that it will take the combined efforts of family and friends to persuade you to spare the monel metal sink, or refrain from decorating the oil burner.

We have tried to give you complete and exact information. The chapter called "General Directions" should be carefully read before starting any project. If you are to restore an antique, we urge you to follow with fidelity the old painting or stenciling best suited to the piece, and to use as far as you can approximate them the antique colors.

Esther Stevens Brazer, famous teacher and pioneer in the field of early American decorative arts, urged that the old traditions be followed in color and pattern. In restoring chairs, trays, and other furniture, she taught her pupils to observe the highest standards of accuracy in working with antique designs. By her scholarly research she made available to the general public patterns which had been lost or forgotten for years. Every person who succumbs to the lure of bronze stenciling owes a debt to Mrs. Brazer and her monumental work, "Early American Decoration."

Your author has gone to many of Mrs. Brazer's sources and, in addition, has sketched designs in the Metropolitan Museum, the Boston Museum, the Philadelphia Museum, and the Museum of the Society for the Preservation of New England Antiquities. Notes have also been taken from private collections and individual owners. The twelve patterns in this book are completely authenticated, with sources tabulated.

Do not feel, however, that in all household decoration you must limit yourself to copying. Be a little daring. Let your imagination spice your work with originality. Try a new idea because you like it, whether or not it has ever been done just that way before.

When we studied design at art school, we learned first that the problem was always to "fill a space in the most pleasing manner." Your tray, chair, or box is your space to fill. It is your "problem." Unless you are actually restoring an antique, do not hesitate to change an old pattern or to try a new one. In the old days artists often changed the standard patterns, making what is known as a "variant." A hundred years ago great-aunt Susie dared to experiment with free-hand painting and stenciling and never hesitated to "vary" a pattern. Your ideas are as good as hers, and some day your "variant" may become a cherished family heirloom. You have much finer materials available to you, and there is keen pleasure in store as you see beauty grow under your finger-tips.

We shall consider in this book two distinct types of decoration, i.e., free-hand painting and stenciling, and since a beginner can achieve satisfactory and even spectacular results with a stencil, we shall discuss it first.

CHAPTER ONE

STENCILING

Stenciling is the transferring of a design by laying a cut-out pattern or "theorem" on a given surface and brushing the cut-out pattern with paint or bronze powder.

The art of stenciling is older than the word itself, for the act of transferring color and form by means of a cut-out pattern seems to have sprung up in the civilizations of many different countries almost simultaneously. Although we are concerned in our work chiefly with bronze stenciling in America in the early and middle nineteenth century, it is interesting to take a brief look at the craft as it has been practised since the days of antiquity. Some stencils remain in very old Buddhist temples. Chinese and Japanese artists combined exquisitely cut stencils with equally exquisite brush strokes, and sometimes it is difficult for an expert to determine which is the stencil and which the brush stroke. In countless cathedrals and churches of Europe stencils were used on walls. The I H S symbol on the Cross was stencilled more often than not. In the simple world of the far Pacific Islands native women are said to have developed primitive stencils for ornamenting clothing by means of piercing leaves and applying color through the holes.

Stenciling has never been a primary art. It has always been a short cut, and in nineteenth-century America was a quick device for obtaining the most decoration for the least effort. When artisans in Europe heard tales of the great Byzantine mosaic wall decorations it is probable that they used the stencil as a makeshift for the intricate mosaics they could not have. Patterns of certain European wall stencils show a distinct Byzantine influence.

In the same way, cabinet makers in America who could not afford time and effort to do the carving and brass work of the Empire period in Europe, satisfied themselves and their patrons by copying many of the metal medallions and acanthus leaf carvings in gilt stenciling. The trade of the "gilders" came into prominence and the art of bronze stenciling grew and grew for nearly one hundred years. William Eaton of New Boston, New Hampshire,

Figure 1. FLOWER BASKET STENCIL

For complete directions for making see Plate I and Chapter I

Thomas Gildersleeve of New York, George Lord of Portland, Maine, are just a few of the famous names prominent in American stenciling. Stencil kits belonging to these old gilders may be seen in certain museums and private collections and there are still extant many of their lovely old stencil patterns.

The word stencil, according to the Encyclopedia Britannica, used to be "stinsil," and is derived from the old French "estinnceller," to sparkle, to powder with stars, an old term in heraldry. How appropriate a derivation for the particular art of bronze stenciling which we shall discuss in this book! Anyone who has worked with the fascinating gold, silver, copper, and even sapphire, red, and green bronze powders available to the modern stenciler, can think of no more fitting background for the word unless it were to be "star-dust."

Because the stencil is so easy to use, it is a boon to women of today. Many a housewife has real creative ability in the field of arts and crafts, but is not trained in painting technique. If she takes a few lessons in applying a stencil, this able housewife can produce almost unbelievable results. There is plenty of scope for her creative ability if she uses the "many-unit" stencil. Her equipment consists of several cut-outs of single grapes, a leaf or two, and a larger circular object which may serve as an apple, a plum, or a peach. Using them and building elaborate designs from such simple units is great fun. Here are some basic cut-outs in a many-unit stencil. Before we start playing with these fascinating objects, however, let us try beginner's luck with a single unit stencil.

Plum   Leaf   Strawberry

Grapes

Further on in this volume there is a chapter on "General Directions," but in order to get you into action without further reading we will let you do a tray at once.

[13]

Patterns in this book may be inexpensively enlarged or reduced to fit your project by having a blueprint or photostat made at any local blue-print shop.

PLATE I. FLOWER BASKET STENCIL

FIGURE 1A

FIGURE 1B

PLATE I. BASKET AND FLOWER DESIGN

The single unit stencil came into general use in the later days of American stenciling, when it became more important to turn out quantity than quality. In the beginning gilders and cabinet makers took pride in the many unit stencil and the variety of patterns they were able to achieve by building up their fruit groups, grape by grape, gaining the effect of a veritable background of foliage by the clever manipulation of one leaf in many different positions.

DIRECTIONS FOR REPRODUCING

Materials: One ten by twelve inch piece of architect's linen, medium soft pencil, sharp pointed embroidery scissors, razor blade, punch, tray, box or other appropriate article on which to transfer the design.

Paints: Artist's oils in tubes, alizarin crimson, Prussian blue, burnt sienna, verdigris (green).

Bronze powders: Brushed brass, silver or aluminum, red, gold-leaf powder or gold powder.

Brushes: Half-inch or three-quarter inch quill brush, mounted on a small stick. Two two-inch brushes about two inches in width, one to be used for background painting and one for varnishing. It pays to buy a good one. Small piece of chamois or pure silk velvet. Tin cigarette box (flat fifty size) containing a square of upholstering velour.

Varnish: A small can of good quality twenty-four-hour varnish.

CUTTING THE PATTERN

Place the architect's linen (dull side up) over the pattern and trace carefully on the linen. Make a hole in each segment of the pattern. Insert scissors in hole and carefully cut out each separate segment of the design. Fine stem lines may be cut with a razor blade or sharp pointed knife. A steel embroidery punch is useful for making small holes. But the holes must be rounded and evened with tips of your scissors. Accurate cutting is important as you will use your stencil over and over again. In your finished cut-out, if any small bridge lines have been snipped by mistake, mend them by pasting Scotch tape on both sides of stencil and recutting the pattern through the double layer of transparent tape.

PREPARING THE MATERIALS

A simple rectangular tray, approximately thirteen by seventeen inches, may be purchased in many of the "dollar" stores or in a hardware store.

This design may also be used on an oval or even a round tray. Blank reproductions of antique trays are on sale at the larger art supply stores and may be ordered by mail. The design is also appropriate for boxes or canisters.

If your tray is shiny, new tin, wash thoroughly with soap and water. Dry carefully and give it a thin coat of shellac. The color of the shellac is unimportant, as we use this simply to prevent rust from forming. After the shellac coat is completely dry, apply two coats of a good quality flat-black paint, at least twenty-four hours apart. When the flat-black background is bone dry, you are ready for the varnish coat on which you will stencil.

Before you apply the varnish it is well to prepare your bronze powders. We find the small tin box from the flat-fifty cigarettes very satisfactory as a receptacle for the powders. A piece of upholstering velvet is cut to fit the box and placed inside. On this mat, pour small mounds of each of the colored bronzes. The box actually becomes a small palette, and after using may be carefully closed and the powders are all ready for use again. Have in readiness your piece of soft chamois or silk velvet. Place this around the tip of your right fore-finger, thus making your finger-tip your instrument for stenciling.

Varnishing Before Stenciling

Pour a small quantity of good quality, twenty-four hour varnish in a saucer and warm slightly. It helps the smoothness of your varnish coat if your tray is also slightly warm and both tray and varnish may be left for a few moments in a warm oven with the gas turned off. You want them to be no more than luke-warm.

Dip your brush completely in the saucer of varnish. Then remove excess fluid by pressing against side of saucer. Working from the center out, apply the varnish in quick strokes, using care to cover every bit of the surface. Try for a thin but evenly coated surface. Allow the varnish to become almost dry. It may take half an hour; it may take two hours, depending on the varnish itself and the amount of moisture in the air on that particular day. If the weather is damp, be sure to work in a room as near seventy degrees or seventy-two degrees as possible. Far better results are obtained on a clear day with little humidity.

After half an hour test the varnish with your finger-tip. It should feel slightly sticky but not sticky enough to hold your finger to the surface. In a short time experience will teach you exactly the right moment to begin stenciling.

STENCILS FROM CUTTING AND MORROW COLLECTION
Print Department, Metropolitan Museum of Art

Place your stencil just where you wish the design to appear. Dip your "velvet" finger gently in the silver dust and rub over the cut-out spaces marked 1. Use a gentle circular motion, working from the edges toward the center. A more interesting effect is obtained if the powder is not applied too solidly. Grapes and leaves, as well as tendrils and stems, may be done in silver. Shake excess silver dust from finger, move the suede or velvet to a fresh surface and dip into the gold leaf powder for the three large flowers, and all parts of the design labeled 2. Rub the centers in first, as you may choose to do the outer petals in red bronze. The basket may now be applied in either gold leaf powder or brushed brass. Finally, tip the outer petals of the flowers, labeled 3, with red bronze.

You are now ready to remove the stencil. Do this with great care so that smudges of metallic powder do not get on your black surface. If your tray, in spite of this, does become smudged with gilt powder, the damage may be repaired by covering the smudges with flat black, being sure to use black from the same can as the background paint. If you do this, your touching up will not show after the final varnish coat is applied.

Allow bronze powders to dry for at least two days. Although they often seem dry in a few hours, when your next coat of varnish is applied it is apt to throw the bronze into solution again. It helps to wipe off excess powder with a damp cloth before varnishing. It really pays good dividends to wait for a full week for the bronze powder to dry before applying the first of the finishing varnish coats.

The use of a variety of bronze colors is optional. This design is handsome when done entirely in brushed brass or gold leaf powder, with overtones of transparent oil paint applied.

Overtones of Oils

In many instances the old gilders used a transparent wash of oil paint to bring out a flower or fruit tone. Colored bronze powders in red, blue, and green, which we may buy commercially, were not available until the middle of the nineteenth century. Many old stencils were done simply in gold.

Alizarin red may be used to tint the flowers; Prussian blue, the grapes; and the leaves may be brightened with a judicious application of green. You will be quite justified, however, if you prefer the simplicity of a plain gold stencil with no coloring whatever. The design may be left just as stenciled in any one of the bronze powders.

In using the oil paints over a gold stencil, mix in a small jar top, one part turpentine and three parts varnish. Add a small quantity of paint and mix with the turpentine and varnish, then apply a clear transparent coat over the well-dried stencil.

Figure 2a is a border unit to use on this tray. Trace and cut the stencil as you did for Figure 1. Mark a border line with white chalk on your tray and move the unit in a repeat pattern along line until entire pattern is completed. Keep centers of leaves slightly dark to suggest veins.

Figure 2b is the corner pattern to be used with this border and may be applied at the four corners of the tray.

If your tray is circular, Figure 2a may be repeated all around the edge of the tray. Mark a circular line in chalk and build your own border out of the single leaf unit. An antique tray with a design very similar to this one had gold and silver only for its color scheme. The flowers and fruit had been delicately accented in transparent oils.

STRIPING

To complete this tray, three rows of striping are painted on the floor of the tray, framing the center pattern. Use a band three-eighths of an inch wide for the middle stripe, flanked on each side by a sixteenth of an inch pin stripe. Since most of the striping on old trays was done in yellow, we use that color frequently in our work. It is very effective in setting the design. First read carefully the section on "Striping" in "General Directions."

Put a teaspoon of varnish and half a teaspoon turpentine into a small jar top. Add equal quantities of chrome yellow medium, yellow ochre with a touch of raw umber.

It is well to lay the wide band first. Make two fine lines on the edges of the three-eighths of an inch band, then fill in the center of band with a medium size sable brush (not a striper).

We always mix our striping paint with a small brush or stick before putting the striping brush into it. When paint is thoroughly mixed with turpentine and varnish dip striping brush in all the way to hilt. Grasp it tightly between thumb and forefinger, steadying it with the third finger and pull it firmly toward you on the line you wish to stripe. Guide with your little finger, and may the angels be with you!

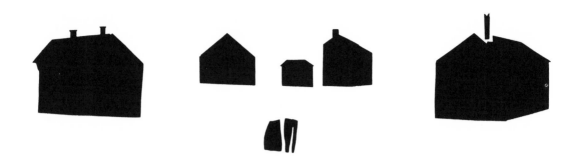

STENCILS FROM CUTTING AND MORROW COLLECTION
Print Department, Metropolitan Museum of Art

CHAPTER TWO

GENERAL DIRECTIONS

This chapter on general directions contains important basic material and should be referred to before starting any project. In it are methods of cutting and applying stencils, techniques for brush-stroke painting, and step by step directions for finishing. Read it carefully and remember that every suggestion is based on experience. When we say "be careful of dust," we are telling you that in our early attempts at furniture decorating we were not careful of dust, blithely supposing that final varnish coats would smooth out rough surfaces. We have found that meticulous care from the first stages makes the final stage of finishing a pleasure instead of a time of chagrin and disappointment. Do not be alarmed at the long list of "materials needed." This kit which you buy will see you through months of decorating. You can paint enough Christmas gifts for the entire family and have enough paint left over for Grandmother's Hitchcock Chair.

BASIC MATERIALS NEEDED

Brushes: A brush two inches wide for background painting. A brush one and one-half to two inches wide for varnishing. It really pays to spend money on this one. A fine quality varnish brush from an art supply store will pay good dividends when you are working for that "satin" finish at the end. Three quill brushes, to be mounted on small sticks, half-inch size; three-quarter inch size; one inch size; one striping brush, one and one-half inches long. Do not mount this one and choose the narrowest one you can find. One medium size sable or camel's hair brush. One very fine sable brush for tiny brush-stroke scrolls.

CARE OF BRUSHES

Never let a brush dry with paint in it. If you are to continue working for several days, you may keep your brushes in a can of turpentine. Some people prefer linseed oil. If it is to be a matter of a week or more before you use your large brushes again, wash them by rubbing them briskly until a suds is formed on a cake of yellow soap with warm water. Rinse under running water until brush is soft and paint free. Small brushes should be cleaned in turpentine and soap and water after each using. It is helpful to keep them wrapped in waxed paper to save them from becoming full of dust. Dust in paint brushes is the bane of all decorators. Try to prevent those dust particles from catching up with you.

Do your large surface flat coats and final varnish coats in a room without rugs such as a bath-room or kitchen. If your large surfaces can dry without becoming contaminated with dirt, the final finishing job will be one of pure joy and satisfaction.

BACKGROUND MATERIALS

Medium size can flat black paint; pint of turpentine. If you plan to paint furniture you may select a good semi-gloss paint in any color, for backgrounds. If furniture is to be stenciled in black, we recommend the flat black paint as a base for stenciling. The finish is built up by several varnish coats.

One-half pint good quality twenty-four-hour varnish, for use in bronze stenciling. One-half pint super valspar or other good four-hour drying varnish. (To be used as alcohol-proof final coat, or to use as base for bronze stenciling if you find yourself working on a damp day.)

Artists Oils in Tubes: Philips white or Permalba; lamp black; Van Dyke brown; American vermilion; alizarin crimson; chrome yellow medium; yellow ochre; chrome green; permanent green; burnt umber; raw umber; ultramarine blue.

Transparent Oils in Tubes: (To use over bronze stenciling) alizarin crimson; yellow lake; Prussian blue; verdigris (green); mauve (purple); burnt sienna (partially transparent).

For Stenciling Bronze Powders: Brushed brass; gold leaf powder (deeper richer gold color than brushed brass); aluminum bronze (silver color); fire bronze (red); green and blue, (seldom used.)

Materials used in Stenciling: Yard of architect's linen; fine pointed embroidery scissors; razor blade or Exacto knife; good quality tracing paper; traceolene (to be used in tracing and keeping old designs which you may acquire from time to time); small piece of chamois or pure silk velvet; black drawing ink; fine drawing pen; small tin cigarette box (flat fifty size); a stick of white chalk and black drawing charcoal.

PREPARATION OF ARTICLES FOR DECORATING

Materials necessary to clean old tin or furniture: Paint remover, rust remover (Rusticide), steel wool, 00 sandpaper, turpentine, paint scraper or putty knife, soap and water.

Brushes: Cheap brush for applying paint remover (do not use it for anything else). Two-inch wide brush for applying ground coat, one and one-half or two-inch wide brush for varnishing.

Paints: A good quality flat paint to be used for all tinware, small objects or furniture on which you plan to stencil. Semi-gloss paint, to be used for background painting of furniture or boxes on which you intend to do brush stroke painting. Starting with a semi-gloss paint cuts down the amount of varnishing necessary in the final finishing. In all cases use at least two coats of paint for base color.

FURNITURE CLEANING

In cleaning furniture for decoration, all paint need not come off if it is in good smooth condition and neither cracked nor peeling. Sand the chair well with 00 sandpaper and smooth down with steel wool before applying background paint.

If base coat is cracked or very uneven, it is better to remove it and strip the piece to the bare wood. Use a good quality paint remover and follow directions on the can. When chair is stripped and dry, sand thoroughly with 00 sandpaper. Be sure your chair or chest is completely clean, with no traces of paint remover, before you start to paint it. If you wash it with soap and water let it become bone dry. Dampness, wax or paint remover left on the surface will lift your new coat of paint.

If wood is soft and porous, it is wise to give your article a coat of shellac before putting on your background paint.

HITCHCOCK CHAIRS

You may paint your furniture any color you choose, but if you are trying to restore a cane or rush-bottom Hitchcock chair, the correct color is a reddish black. This color is achieved by giving the chair a first coat of

Figure 2. CHAIR STENCILED BY ESTHER STEVENS BRAZER
Owned by Mrs. Wayne Thompson, Winchester, Mass.
Courtesy Museum of the Society for the Preservation of New England Antiquities

Chinese red paint. (This may be semi-gloss, but not high-gloss.) When this coat is thoroughly dry, apply flat black, thinned down with turpentine. Allow the wide main slat, which will take the largest unit of the design, to dry black. Now the fun begins for you, as you attempt to imitate wood-graining in your chair by wiping out the black paint so that a gleam of red under-coat shows. Your first attempts should be by the trial and error method. Have a large cloth at hand to wipe off your graining if it does not please you at first. To do the graining, you may use crumpled mosquito netting, newspaper, a dry brush or any one of a number of other things. The idea is to go over your wet, black paint with some object that will remove just enough paint to give the effect of grained wood as the red paint shows up underneath. We have found a yard of mosquito netting the most effective. When you have secured a graining which you like, let it dry. It will seem very dull in finish when it first dries, due to the dull finish of the flat black paint. After varnishing, however, it will be much more attractive. Your chair or chest is now ready for bronze stenciling.

Some of the finest Hitchcock type chairs were painted to imitate rose-wood and have a beautiful rosy-brown finish. In this instance, the brown paint is put on the chair first, rubbed off and the red coat is put over the brown. It is a very complicated process and we do not recommend it for beginners.

Tin Trays and Other Painted Tin

If the tray is an old one, and has even a little of the antique design left on it, try to have the design recorded by an expert in tray painting. It is a pity to obliterate a fine old design by over-painting.

If the tray is old and rusty with no design, remove dirt and rust with paint remover, steel wool and Rusticide. Do not attempt to paint over rust as it will eat its way through the paint and ruin your design. Be sure to remove all traces of paint remover with Carbona and soap and water before putting your ground coat on. It is equally important to have your article absolutely dry before starting to paint.

After cleaning your tray or other article, get a ground coat on as quickly as possible as rust can begin again in a few days. We have found a coat of shellac an excellent sealer coat before applying the flat paint. After shellac is thoroughly dry, give the object two coats of flat paint twenty-four hours apart. You are now ready to begin to decorate.

EARLY STENCILED TRAY, *circa* 1840, SHOWING DOUBLE BORDER
From the Author's Collection

EARLY STENCILED TRAY, *circa* 1820
Courtesy Dr. Warren Stearns, Billerica, Mass.

[26]

Cutting the Pattern: Place the architect's linen (dull side up) over the pattern and trace carefully the whole design on the linen. There is no need to trace the numbers on the pattern. They are merely used as a color guide in the original pattern.

Punch a small hole in the center of each separate segment of the pattern. Use an ordinary commercial punch to make these holes, or you may prefer a quick jab of your fine scissors. Place the scissors in the incision and cut out each segment of the design. Discard cut-out pieces. Be careful not to snip the little bridge lines between the segments. Use small scissors with sharp pointed blades. Curved lines may be cut with manicure scissors. Some people prefer to use a razor blade or a sharp jack-knife. It is not important which method you use, so long as you make a neat job of cutting out each segment, because it is through these cut-outs that your design is transferred.

<table>
<tr><td>Stencil as it looks after tracing on architect's linen</td><td>Stencil as it looks after segments of pattern have been cut out. Held against black background</td></tr>
</table>

When the cutting on your stencil is completed, the piece of architect's linen should still measure 10 x 12 inches, with the design perforated on it by the cutting out of each segment of the pattern. Test your stencil by placing it on a piece of black paper or dark cloth. The entire design should show through the cut-out holes as if it were a silhouette. In your finished cut-out, if any small bridge lines were snipped by mistake, they may be mended by pasting the Scotch tape as a brace both back and front, then re-cutting the segment through the double Scotch tape.

PREPARATION OF BRONZE POWDERS

A very small quantity of bronze powder or gold dust is actually used in stenciling. To avoid waste, the powders may be held over from one stenciling to another. We find the small tin box from the flat fifty cigarettes a satisfactory receptacle for the powders. A piece of upholsterer's velour is cut to fit the box. On this mat, pour small mounds of each of the colored bronze powders. The box actually becomes a palette, and after using, it may be carefully closed and the powders are ready for use again.

VARNISHING BEFORE STENCILING

Pour a small quantity of twenty-four-hour varnish in a saucer and warm ever so slightly. It helps the smoothness of your coat if tray is also slightly warm. Dip your brush completely in the saucer of varnish and remove excess fluid by pressing brush gently against side. Working from the center of the tray outwards, apply the varnish in quick light strokes, using care to cover every bit of the surface. Try for a thinly coated even surface. If varnish is lumpy or seems to jell a little, strain it through an old nylon stocking.

Allow varnish to become almost dry. It may take twenty minutes; it may take an hour and a half, depending on the varnish itself and the amount of moisture in the air on that particular day. If it is a really damp or humid day, postpone your varnishing if possible. In any case, the room temperature should be at least seventy degrees. If it is a rainy day and you *must* varnish, use four-hour quick drying varnish rather than the twenty-four-hour variety.

After half an hour, test the varnish with your finger tip. It should feel slightly sticky but not wet enough to hold your finger to the surface. Experience will soon teach you exactly the right moment to begin stenciling.

Care of Stencils

Always wipe stencil clean with Carbona or other dress cleaning fluid after using. No bronze powder should be allowed to remain on either front or back of stencil. Place your stencil on your varnished tray or chair or box in exactly the spot where you wish the design to appear.

Wrap the forefinger of your right hand in the silk velvet or soft chamois, taking care that all raw edges are tucked under. Dip "velvet finger" gently in bronze dust. You are now ready for the exciting moment of transferring the gold powder to the design. Using a gentle circular motion, rub the bronze-coated velvet finger over the cut-out section of the stencil. Work from the outer edges of hole toward center to avoid spilling gold powder under edges of design. Do not fill large cut-out sections of pattern solidly, but allow powder to fade out as you approach center. This will give a moulded effect to fruit and flowers which is attractive. Stems, tendrils or geometric units should be solidly filled, however. It is better to use too little than too much powder, so take it gently!

When you have completed the bronzing process, remove your stencil with great care, to avoid blowing the excess bronze powder on the damp varnish. If, in spite of care, you do smudge your background, you may remove the damage after varnish is bone dry by touching up your mistakes with flat black. Use paint from the same can as your background, and on applying the second coat of varnish your retouching will not be detected.

Striping

Everything is fun in tray and chair painting except striping, and even that is fun when you learn how to do it.

Mix one teaspoon clear twenty-four-hour varnish and one-half teaspoon of turpentine in a jar top about two inches in diameter. Squeeze an inch or so of paint from tube and blend thoroughly in varnish and turpentine with a wooden stick. When paint is completely dissolved and the consistency of heavy cream, you are ready to begin.

Immerse a quill striping brush (one and a half inches long and as thin a brush as you can buy) into the paint all the way up to the quill. Press out excess paint gently and test the brush by pulling across a piece of paper, drawing the brush toward the body. Hold brush between the thumb and first two fingers, steadying it with the remaining fingers. Now place brush gently on your surface and paint the narrow stripe by pulling brush toward the body. If the line wavers, wipe it off, relax, and try again. Since the flat black surface is not an easy one to remove paint from, striping is more easily done if you varnish the surface first. You may wipe out striping mistakes with impunity if you are striping on a dry varnished surface.

Most striping on trays and black chairs or other furniture is done in yellow. One part chrome yellow medium, one part yellow ochre dulled with Van Dyke brown, mixed with two parts varnish and one part turpentine, makes a good striping color.

On light furniture the striping is most often done in black, although dark blue-green or vermilion striping is sometimes seen. If you are a beginner, the wider striping is best accomplished by drawing two hair-line stripes for the outside edge sand filling in the center with a medium sized sable brush (not a striping brush). Even in bronze stenciling the yellow stripe is used, although sometimes bronze powder is dusted over the wide stripe when it is almost dry.

TRANSFERRING THE PATTERN

A good tough tracing paper from an art supply store is essential for transferring the pattern to the object to be painted. Trace the pattern from the book, using a medium soft pencil. If design is to be transferred to a *black* background, cover the reverse side of tracing paper with chalk. Place pattern chalk side down on the tray, box, or other object in the spot where you wish it to appear. Some people use masking tape to hold the design in place. If one works carefully, however, the design may be held in place with the left hand. Allow enough time to transfer the entire pattern at one sitting, because unless the tracing paper is anchored in place it will slip if you leave it. Draw over each line of tracing on the unchalked side to transfer the pattern. If the pattern is to be used on a *light* background, soft black pencil or drawing charcoal is used on the reverse side of stencil instead of white chalk. The design is then transferred by drawing over the pattern in pencil on the unmarked side.

Make a tracing of the pattern from the book. With a ruler, divide the entire pattern into one-inch squares by means of horizontal and vertical lines. On another sheet of tracing paper make the same number of squares either one and one-half inches or two inches wide, depending on whether you wish to enlarge the pattern half again as much, or twice as much. You will find that using the squares as a guide, you can draw the pattern accurately in the larger size.

To reduce the size of a pattern, make a tracing from the book and mark off the tracing in two inch squares. On another sheet of tracing paper make one-inch squares, or one and one-half inch squares if you want your finished pattern to be three-quarters as large rather than half as large. Draw the pattern from the original tracing, using the squares as guiding lines.

If a design in this book is too large or too small for the space where you plan to use it, a photostat or blueprint may be made from any drawing in the book at small cost. By this photostat process the design can be enlarged or reduced to suit your purpose without effort on your part, eliminating the need of a pantograph or squared paper.

THE "ANTIQUE" FINISH

Many pieces of painted tin and other painted furniture are ruined by too heavy an application of burnt umber or other colors to give the effect of age and antiquity. Observation of many old trays has convinced us that the old tray painters did very little to dull their pigments, and a bright hard finish was undoubtedly the accepted thing for trays, chairs, and other painted objects. A small amount of burnt umber added to the first two or three varnish coats will dull the bright pigments somewhat. The final coat of varnish, however, should be clear.

If some portion of the design seems too bright, if one piece of fruit or a flower seems to "jump out" of place, a small amount of burnt umber on the tip of the finger, rubbed over the offending part of the pattern will break the bright finish and put it back into place. The paint must be hard and dry before you apply this "toning" treatment.

In removing the "new" look from a chair, chest or a large piece of furniture which is painted some other color than black, an effect of age may be achieved by mixing a slightly darker tone of the original color by adding black.   Burnt umber or Van Dyke brown should be used if the object is yellow, tan, or cream color.   With a soft cloth wipe on this darker tone. The article must be bone dry.   Allow the darker tone to penetrate corners, turnings and crevices of the piece.   With a dry cloth wipe off the darker tone you have just applied, leaving a light film over most of the piece.   The darker tones remain in corners and mouldings or turnings.

After this is dry apply a thin coat of varnish, and when dry rub down with rotten stone and crude oil for the final finish.

Another method of dulling colors which seem too bright is to wash the design before applying any varnish coats with a weak solution of ammonia water.   Two teaspoons of ammonia in one cup of water will give you the proper solution.   This ammonia and water should be washed over the dry design once a day for several days.

Time will dull your tray with no help from anyone, and a final admonition on the subject of "antique" finishing is to use more restraint than burnt umber.

Color

You should know something of the artists' oils in tubes which will be mentioned from time to time in this book.   After you have become familiar with the colors mentioned in this book, experiment with them by mixing. Certain ones will combine well; others, when put together, will give a disastrous effect.   It will be amusing for you to try out various combinations and learn for yourself that red and green will neutralize each other and become gray or black.   Alizarin crimson mixed with white becomes light pink.   Many different tints and shades may be achieved by using your imagination.

This section on "Color" is merely to interpret certain trade names and to give you an idea of what to expect when you squeeze paint from a tube.

The "transparent" colors are the ones used most in stenciling.   The reason for this is that when they are thinned out with varnish and applied over the bronze stenciling the stencil is still visible, although tinted with the new color.

The "opaque" oil colors, on the contrary, are heavier, and when applied give a thick surface which conceals any pattern which may be beneath it.

The transparent colors are as follows: Alizarin crimson, a deep clear red; Prussian blue, blue with a slightly greenish cast; yellow lake, a light lemon yellow; verdigris, a bright aqua-tinted green; mauve, dark violet;

burnt sienna, (semi-transparent) reddish brown or rust color; raw umber, brownish yellow color, used to take "new" look from over-bright pigments.

The opaque colors are as follows: Chrome yellow medium, very bright yellow; yellow ochre, yellow leaning toward tan; Van Dyke brown, dark brown, semi-transparent; chrome green, dull green, almost olive; permanent green, pure rather bright green; American vermilion, bright pure red; ultramarine blue, deep full blue; Philips white and permalba, thick heavy white; lampblack, black.

BRUSH-STROKE PAINTING

Brush-stroke painting requires more training and technique than stenciling. It took old-time furniture painters years of practice, from the time they were boyhood apprentices, to perfect the delicate "one stroke" painting which we admire today. Do not grieve too much, therefore, if your first attempt to do a border of leaves with swift sure brush action disappoints you. It is rather like learning a tennis stroke. It is more important to make your stroke correctly than to get your ball over the net, or your leaf curled without a wiggle.

Three quill brushes in assorted sizes, with the major brush about three-fourths of an inch long, are necessary. These quills may be fitted over the handle of an old paint brush or small wooden stick.

Try out your new brushes by covering several pages of drawing paper with brush-stroke borders of various sizes and shapes. Try them all.

[33]

It is important to have your paint mixed correctly. Put two teaspoons of varnish and one of turpentine in a mason jar top. Squeeze in an inch or so of yellow ochre or American vermilion or verdigris. Mix very thoroughly. Dip your brush in, and fill to the brim with paint, squeezing out excess paint on side of jar top. From the minute you take up your paint-filled brush, begin to relax. Brush strokes are fun if you really let yourself go, but brush strokes timidly executed with some touching back are not worth putting on the poorest object.

Place your brush, well filled with paint, on the paper and let it puddle for the thick part of the stroke, narrowing your line to a hair as you complete the stroke by lifting brush from paper. Paint discarded tin cans black, and practise leaf and line borders so that you will get a feeling for working on a circular surface . . . and do not forget to relax your wrist as you work. Relax your entire body too; it helps!

FINISHING

The fine art of finishing a tray or other painted object is one which takes infinite patience and pains. There is none of the excitement of seeing a design grow under your lively fingers, none of the thrill of seeing the stencil take shape as you dip your velvet sponge into gold dust, but in the satin smooth finish built up with painstaking care through at least six processes, lies a magic charm.

It is wasted effort to finish one tray at a time. We find best results may be obtained by bringing five or six trays to the varnish stage at once. Then plan to devote at least half an hour a day for a week or two to bring them up to a durable, permanent finish. Use a good bar varnish or other slow drying varnish. Proper weather conditions will aid you almost as much as a good brush, but both are important. Do *not* expect to achieve promising results by varnishing on a rainy or misty, moisty day.

STEP I. Have your trays in an absolutely dust-free condition. Washing them in warm water and soap and drying with a lintless towel is a good beginning. It is often a good idea, if varnishing on a chilly day, to place the trays and varnish in a luke-warm oven *with the heat turned off*.

STEP II. Pour enough varnish from the can into a small container. Old jar tops are good for this. Enough varnish for six medium size trays is about two ounces.

STEP III. After trying out the dry brush on your hand to remove any loose hairs, dip it in your varnish and give three or four brush strokes on practice paper or tin to distribute varnish evenly through the brush.

Step IV.   Put a *thin* coat of varnish on your tray.   This is not fun. It is ever so much more exciting to slather the varnish on and wipe up the bubbles with your brush.   This method, however, will not give you a fine, ultimate finish on your tray.   Begin in the middle and work out to the edges with the thinnest coat of varnish that will cover every inch of your tray.

Step V.   Allow to *dry*.   Twenty-four hours will usually do this, but if the weather changes and becomes full of moisture, it may take longer.

You will be sorry if you try to put a second coat of varnish on before the first one is bone dry.   If you do, however, and the whole pattern "slides," clean up the sad mess with Carbona.   When your tray is dry, put on a second thin coat of varnish.

Step VI.   After the second varnish is hard, rub *gently* with steel wool or 00 sandpaper, and I mean *gently*.

Step VII: Give two more thin coats of varnish, twenty-four hours, at least, apart.

Step VIII.   Now rub your whole tray with powdered pumice and water. Place pumice in a saucer.   Dip cotton in water and wring out.   Rub cotton in pumice and then over the tray, being especially careful to pumice the crease between floor and sides of tray.

Step IX.   Give it two more coats of thin varnish and when thoroughly dry, rub gently with "wet and dry" sandpaper and water.   If you cannot obtain wet and dry sandpaper at your hardware store, substitute rotten-stone and water for this step.

Step X.   As a final coat use super valspar.   It is heat proof and alcohol proof.   Rub to a soft finish by dipping cotton in crude oil, then in rotten-stone and polishing to a satin smoothness.

Satin Varnish

The dull finish or "satin" varnish put out by many paint companies makes a satisfactory finish for chairs, chests and other large pieces of furniture.   It does not require rubbing down.   For trays or boxes and other small wares, we recommend the slower but handsomer finish of rubbing down a good bar varnish with pumice or rottenstone until a glowing patina has been achieved.   As a final coat for trays, super valspar will give a durable and alcohol-proof finish.

Do not try for too dull a finish on your trays. Some of the very hand-some early trays had an almost high gloss finish. One of the trays photo-graphed in this book, which to the best of our knowledge is over a hundred years old, has not been revarnished, and yet it is not really dull. It is possible that the old tray makers strove for a bright, hard finish and did little rubbing down.

PEAR DESIGN FOR MINIATURE TRAY

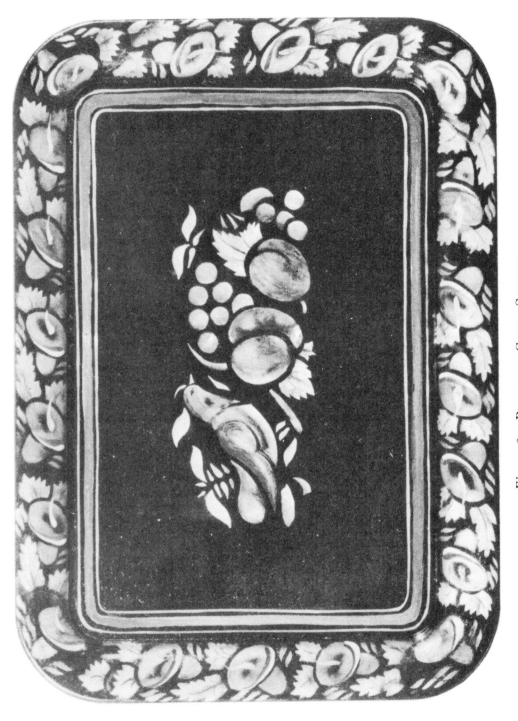

Figure 2. Bird and Calla Stencil

For complete directions for making see Plate II and Chapter III

Chapter Three

SINGLE AND DOUBLE UNIT STENCIL PATTERNS

Plate II. BIRD AND CALLA LILY

The stencil patterns used on the tray were cut directly from sketches of a Pennsylvania Dutch chair dated 1825, in the Metropolitan Museum. Overpainting is applied to the stencil for color, and the design is equally amusing on a tray, box or chair. The original color scheme is followed because it is such an attractive one. Although the chair itself is dark brown in background color, we have taken the liberty of using black as background in adapting the pattern for a tray.

The bird is the main motif in the large slat at back of chair; the calla lily is the design used on the center slat and the yellow and green striping, which we have adapted to use on the tray, is used to outline the form of the chair. If you care to try this pattern on a chair, we recommend the mottled brown in the original, as background color. A set of six chairs in this color scheme would be charming, used with a drop-leaf table in either maple or walnut.

DIRECTIONS FOR STENCILING

Although any size tray may be used, the design has been adapted to fit the standard oblong size seventeen and one-half by twelve and three-fourths. Give the tray two coats of flat black paint, twenty-four hours apart, and while waiting for it to dry, cut your stencil.

CUTTING THE STENCIL

Read "General Directions" on stenciling in Chapter Two. Trace patterns for stencils directly on architect's linen and cut stencils carefully. It always seems easier to us to cut the small units first.

APPLYING THE STENCIL

Give your tray, which has become thoroughly dry, a thin coat of varnish. When varnish reaches "tacky" stage, place bird stencil in position

PLATE II. BIRD AND CALLA LILY

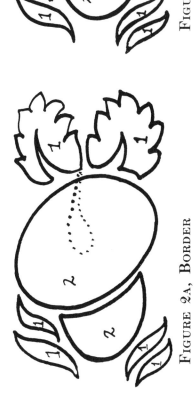

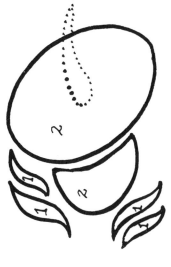

Parts of design marked 1 are stencilled in silver.

Parts marked 2 are stencilled in brushed brass.

Stamens shown in dotted lines are painted afterwards in bright yellow.

FIGURE 2

FIGURE 2B, CORNER

FIGURE 2A, BORDER

and apply bronze powder. The bird is done in brushed brass, except for his breast, which is silver color. Brushed brass is also used for the large fruit and stem pieces, marked 2. Silver color powder is used for grapes and leaves, marked 1.

The calla lily border uses brushed brass for the lily and silver for leaves. In this stencil, since it is to be overpainted, particular care must be taken to leave shadows as you work. Allow the powder to fade off as you approach the center of the stencil space. Leave center of calla flower quite dark and blurred, stenciling the gold dust close to the edges.

In doing fruits, always rub in a high light in upper right side of both rounded sections to suggest solidity and roundness.

OVERPAINTING

The overpainting on this tray is optional; you may choose to use it with only the bronze powders. A more informal but equally delightful tray results if you follow the plan and color scheme of the original old design.

Using a mixture of two parts varnish to one part turpentine as a sizing base, mix Prussian blue with a speck of ultramarine and paint large fruit forms. Wipe high lights out on right side of both sections of plums. You actually wipe out almost half the color you have put on, allowing the gold powder to show through. Color grapes with same blue used for plums. This blue is used on shoulder and lower right half of wing of bird.

For the leaves in both border and center section, use verdigris, toned down with a little raw umber. Veining may be suggested in the leaves by three fine lines in Van Dyke brown mixed with burnt sienna.

To paint bird, mix small amount of Van Dyke brown and burnt sienna and paint upper left shoulder, top of head and left side of wing, letting color fade out. Wipe out high light on wing between blue and brown. Accent the eye in Van Dyke brown darkened with a little lampblack.

To give depth and form to the calla lily in the border, shade each flower with a brown line to the right of center, following the contour of the edge. After brown line is dry, paint another line beneath it in yellow, brightened with a little Philips white. These two lines give a look of reality which is completed by painting one stamen in the center of each lily in the spot indicated by dotted lines.

If in your stenciling you have left a dark shadow in the center of each lily, the stamen will show up well and set off the design. The shape and size of the stamen is indicated in Figure 4b.

An attractive effect is gained by keeping the leaves in both border and main design in silver and outlining the veins in burnt sienna.

Striping

Read instructions for striping in "General Directions."

Two hairline bands in yellow and a three-eighths-inch band in green, between the two yellow stripes, complete the design on the tray.

For the green stripe mix chrome green and raw umber, darkening it with a little lampblack. Lay the broad stripe first, outlining the edges with a fine quill striping brush and filling in center part with a medium size sable brush. Always stripe toward you. If your line wavers or is uneven, wipe out immediately with a lintless cloth and start over again.

It is best to allow your wide stripe to dry before attempting the two hairline stripes, as you can guide your brush better if you do not have to avoid a wet center stripe. Paint fine stripes in yellow. When striping is done, you are ready to put the finishing coats of varnish on the tray. Complete directions for "finishing" will be found in Chapter II on "General Directions."

Plate III. THE WISTARIA STENCIL

The original cutting of this graceful stencil is from the "Cutting and Morrow" collection in the Metropolitan Museum in New York, and is on file with many other nineteenth century stencils from the same firm. It is not an "early" stencil but falls in the period where delicate and elaborate designs were made in a single unit. The early stencils, built up with care and patience from several theorems, took infinitely more time and skill. As mass production came into vogue, those stencils which could be applied in one operation superseded the others.

These one unit designs were intricate and charming, and cut with the greatest care and precision. They erred often in being over-elaborate, but the workmanship and cutting were exquisite. Since there is no doubt that they speeded up the process of decorating, and since the buying public was not too discriminating, they became immensely popular.

The single leaf or fruit unit repeated over and over to build the design

FIGURE 3

FIGURE 3B

FIGURE 3A

Stamens in gold leaf.
Petals and leaves marked 2 in brushed bras
Wistaria marked 1 in silver.

PLATE III. WISTARIA STENCIL

gave, however, a more beautiful effect. This is why it is often said that by 1850 bronze stenciling had become decadent.

Directions for Reproducing Figure 3.

Preparation of Box. This stencil is very adaptable and may be used on a chair, box or larger piece of furniture. In choosing a box, select one of wood or tin twelve by nine inches long. For this one we used a background color called barn red. Chinese red is equally attractive. Apply two coats with an interval of twenty-four hours between coats.

Step I. *Cutting the Stencil:* Read section on "Stencil Cutting" in chapter "General Directions." Trace designs from Figure 3, Figure 3a and Figure 3b directly on architect's linen, and carefully cut the stencils. Figure 3 has particularly narrow bridges and care must be taken to snip very gently to avoid cutting the partitions.

Step II. *Applying the Stencil:* Apply a thin coat of varnish to top of box. When varnish is almost dry, but still has some adhesiveness left, it is ready for stenciling. Experience will teach you when this crucial moment has been reached.

Step III. *Painting:* Apply large stencil, Figure 3, in exact center of box top. Rub in stamens of flowers in gold-leaf powder. Petals of large flowers and forget-me-nots are done in brushed brass. The wistaria is in silver color. Place the corner motif Figure 3a at each of four corners of box. In the corner motifs, the center circle is stenciled in gold-leaf powder and the small leaves in silver. Allow top of box to dry for twenty-four hours or more and when thoroughly dry, wipe off excess powder with damp cloth.

Step IV. Varnish sides of box. When varnish is ready for stenciling, apply Figure 3b at each end, with center circle in gold and leaves in silver. Gold may also be used for small tulip motif. For front of box, apply Figure 3b in center. Then place tip of stencil at each end of motif and apply silver powder to extend its length. (See illustration.)

Step V. *Striping:* Read section on "Striping" in chapter "General Directions." With a striping brush, add a fine line in yellow around top of box one-half inch in from edge. Around sides of box add a fine stripe in yellow, one-half inch up from bottom.

This striping is entirely optional. If you are adept enough in using the striping brush with bronze powders and varnish, which is more difficult than with oil paint, the border is attractive done in bronze.

Figure 3. WISTARIA STENCIL FROM THE CUTTING AND MORROW COLLECTION
Courtesy Metropolitan Museum of Art, New York City
For diagram for making see complete directions in Chapter III

Figure 4. MEDALLION TRAY
Courtesy Museum of the Society for the Preservation of New England Antiquities
For working diagram see Plate IV.   For complete directions for making see Chapter III

Step VI. *Finishing:* Read section on "Finishing" in chapter "General Directions." To finish give a coat of varnish to which has been added a small amount of raw umber. This tones down the red background color and gives a slight effect of antiquity. We are very much against heavy "antiquity." Too much brown pigment rubbed into a fine fresh design gives a muddy effect. Let time be your "antique man" with only a small amount of help from raw umber, burnt sienna, and lampblack.

The second coat of varnish, applied after the first is completely dry, should be clear. A soft sheen is achieved by rubbing the box, when dry, with rotten-stone and crude oil.

PLATE IV. MEDALLION TRAY

This quaint old tray is distinctive not only because of the medallion repeat used for the border but because of the wandering scrollwork of punched pin holes meandering around the outside edge of the pattern. The original tray is in the museum of the "Society for the Preservation of New England Antiquities." The color scheme is simple since the entire pattern is worked out in brushed brass, gold-leaf powder and silver. There is evidence that the flowers were overpainted in alizarin and that a faint wash of verdigris (green) was applied over the large leaf form. The centers of the medallions are accented with a line of burnt sienna. The date of the tray is circa 1850.

CUTTING THE STENCIL

Trace pattern directly from book on architect's linen. In cutting the stencil, it is somewhat easier to cut small units first, then larger leaves and finally the pin-prick scroll. For the scroll use a large hat pin and make holes carefully and of uniform size. You will notice that the pattern for only one medallion is given. This one unit is repeated over and over again to make the border.

PREPARATION OF TRAY

Select a rectangular tray approximately seventeen and one-half by twelve and three-fourths inches. It may be purchased in any large dollar store and usually comes enameled in bright colors. Wipe tray clean and give it two coats of flat black paint, allowing it to dry for at least twenty-four

COLOR CHART
1. Gold-leaf powder
2. Brushed brass
3. Silver

FIGURE 4

FIGURE 4C

FIGURE 4B

FIGURE 4A

PLATE IV. MEDALLION TRAY

hours between coats. Do not be lured into painting on your flat black surface too soon. This particular paint *seems* to dry in a very short time but actually is not wholly dry for twenty to twenty-four hours.

STENCILING

Give tray a thin coat of good quality bar varnish. Brush your strokes lightly over the tray, taking care to cover every bit of surface but avoiding a too full brush which will put too much varnish on your tray. The thinner the coat the better base for stenciling, but every speck of the tray must be covered.

After half an hour or so, test varnish with tip of finger. When surface is ready for stenciling it should feel slightly adhesive but not really sticky. "Tacky" is the word which has been used to describe it.

Place Figure 4 exactly in center of tray. Hold carefully in position with left hand and apply bronze powder with finger tip wrapped in velvet. The center of the flowers should be done in gold-leaf powder with petals in brushed brass. Large leaf unit is brushed brass and tiny leaves and stems may be done in silver. If, while stenciling, your varnish should become too dry to hold the metallic powders you should wait twenty-four hours and varnish again, then proceed with stenciling as before.

In applying the border, careful manipulation is necessary to make the medallions come out exactly even. The circles at the end must be placed very close together while those at the sides are about three-eighths of an inch apart. Your border may be completely done in brushed brass as you may make it a little more interesting by using silver for the centers.

We have found it most satisfactory to start with the center medallion at the end of the tray and after it is stenciled in position, apply two more on each side of it about an eighth of an inch apart. This makes five circles at each end of tray.

Next place a medallion in center of long border and place three on each side of it, three-eighths of an inch apart. This makes seven circles on each side. Border is completed by stenciling segment of pattern between medallions, using Figure 4b, three petal segment for long sides and Figure 4c, two petal segment for ends. Try to place evenly so that the outer border on the extreme edge of tray is a continuous scalloped edge. After all stenciling has become thoroughly dry, wipe off excess bronze powder with a damp cloth.

ORIGINAL TRAY FROM THE AUTHOR'S COLLECTION
For working diagram see Plate V, Parts 1 and 2
"Courtship Design"

To complete the design and accent the rectangular lines of your tray, you should add three stripes in yellow around the floor of the tray. The center band is three-eighths inch wide and is flanked on each side by a one-sixteenth inch narrow stripe in the same color. In chapter on "General Directions" read section on "Striping" and carefully lay your stripes as indicated. To make the correct yellow, put a scant teaspoon of varnish and one-half teaspoon turpentine in a small container. Squeeze out equal amounts yellow ochre and chrome yellow. Tone down brilliance of color with a dash of Van Dyke brown. Mix thoroughly with small wooden stick to the consistency of heavy cream, and your striping mixture is ready.

Plate V. COURTSHIP TRAY

Although this is an old tray owned and restored by the writer, the central motif was so badly damaged that several units from other sources had to be added to complete the design. It was clear that there was a dog, trees and flowers and the figures of a man and woman. The design as it is restored, then, has really been reassembled. The sketches used in restoring the tray were made in the Metropolitan Museum in New York. The dimensions of the antique tray are twenty-two by sixteen and one-half. The central design will also fit the standard oblong tray seventeen and one-half by twelve and three-quarters. Two border designs are given: one to fit the larger tray which is the original border, and similar design adapted to the narrower border. Prepare your tray by giving it two coats of flat black paint, twenty-four hours apart.

Cutting the Stencil

STEP I: Two "theorems" are needed to reproduce this pattern. The first is called the master theorem and contains the largest part of the pattern. The second contains such items as buttons on the man's coat, his trousers, the stripes on the girl's skirt, and the dog's tongue. For the master theorem, select a piece of architect's linen twelve by nine and one-half inches in size. Place over Figure 5 and draw very carefully. Then cut out the stencil. Next, on a piece of linen seven by six inches in size trace Figure 5a and cut. Finally, trace Figure 5b if you are doing the large tray, as this border fits it. Trace and cut Figure 5c for border for small tray. Figure 5d is a connecting unit in the border which will fit either tray, so it should be

THIS IS THE MASTER THEOREM

Cut out all parts except those shaded by diagonal lines

PLATE V, PART I. COURTSHIP DESIGN

FIGURE 5

FIGURE 5B

BORDER FOR LARGE TRAY

Place Figure 5e in center and repeat 5b at left and right

CORNER MOTIF

FIGURE 5E

FIGURE 5D

BORDER FOR SMALL TRAY

FIGURE 5C

FIGURE 5A

PLATE V, PART II. COURTSHIP DESIGN

cut whichever border you use. Figure 5e is the corner unit and may be used for either size tray.

STENCILING

STEP II: Put a thin coat of varnish on tray. When varnish is almost dry, place master theorem (Figure 5) in center and apply bronze powder. Use silver for faces of man and girl, and for girl's apron and the birds. Stencil the remainder in brushed brass.

Working carefully to avoid spreading bronze dust, place Figure 5a over stencil, fitting hat to headband, skirt to girl, and tongue to dog. Stencil Figure 5a entirely in silver. Allow to dry for forty-eight hours, then wash excess bronze powder off with damp cloth.

PAINTING

STEP III. Pour a teaspoonful of varnish into bottle cap and thin with few drops of turpentine. Squeeze a small amount of alizarin crimson into it. Mix thoroughly and apply thin coating of paint to girl's bodice and skirt, allowing the bronze paint to show through.

Paint flowers in basket, in the bouquet and on bushes at each side with alizarin. The old-fashioned way was to put a light wash of color over the whole flower, making no effort to paint each petal separately. Leave one or two flowers on the bushes to be painted in blue. Tint the cheeks of both girl and boy with alizarin. Paint roof of cottage in alizarin. Mix in a separate cup, Prussian blue with varnish and turpentine, and lightly paint in boy's trousers and top hat. Wipe out a high light on left side of hat and at left of each leg. Tint remaining flowers blue. In the border, large flower motifs are red and the smaller ones blue. The corner motif is red, while the connecting motif, Figure 5d, is not tinted but left in the gold color.

Mix chrome green, permanent green and a small amount of white with varnish and turpentine, and add a few extra leaves among the gold ones on the trees, using a free brush stroke. Paint in extra green leaves in girl's basket, and with many small brush strokes give the suggestion of green grass growing among the cobblestones on the ground. Extend ground line one inch beyond flower bushes by broken parallel lines in green.

Paint leaves in border with verdigris, using no white. In these leaves the bronze color should show through. If green paint seems thick, thin it with a little turpentine. Mix chrome yellow with white and put a dot in center of blue forget-me-nots and other small flowers, after paint is dry.

Draw features in faces with pen and black ink.

STRIPING

A three-eighths-inch wide band is flanked by two fine stripes and is painted on floor of tray one-eighth inch in from the sides.

Read instructions for striping in Chapter "General Directions."

Mix one teaspoon varnish thinned with turpentine in paint cup and add chrome yellow medium and small quantity of raw umber. Stir until paint is entirely dissolved in varnish. Dip striping brush into paint until brush is full. Make two or three trial strokes, then paint broad stripe. Draw outer edges of stripe with striping brush and fill in with medium size sable brush. Allow this broad stripe to dry, then, holding your breath, apply the fine striping on each side.

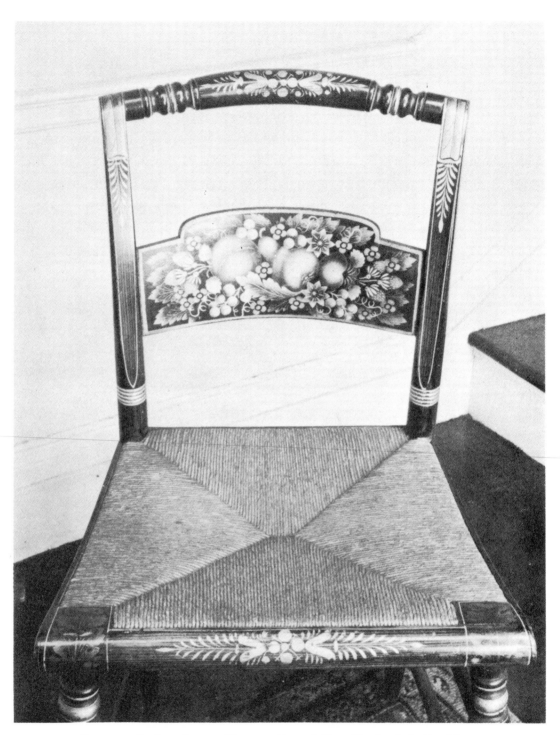

Courtesy Society for the Preservation of New England Antiquities
For complete directions for making, read Chapter IV
For working diagram, see Plate VI

[54]

CHAPTER FOUR

PLATE VI. THE BUILT-UP STENCIL

This stencil is taken from the broad slat of a fine Hitchcock chair in the Museum of the Society for the Preservation of New England Antiquities in Boston. The chair was once owned by Janet Waring, whose book "Early American Stencils on Walls and Furniture" is one of the great works in its field. Although this design is a very elaborate one for beginners, the units are so particularly good that we are including it. The single units may be used to build up simple designs as well as the more intricate one used on the chair. In reproducing this design a skeleton pattern or "theorem" is used, with only a few of the units cut out. The base of the strawberries, the centers of the flowers, the "eye" of the pear and the veins of the leaves are cut first and become the guide or "master theorem" for placing the various fruit units. The entire design on the chair measures twelve and one-half inches across. Due to the smaller size of this page we are giving you a full scale drawing of two-thirds of the pattern (Figure 6). The final third is a separate drawing but may be easily fitted to the rest of the pattern (Figure 6a.) Your "theorem" is composed of Figure 6 and Figure 6a matched together and cut as a single unit.

DESIGN FOR LARGE SLAT ON HITCHCOCK CHAIR

Step I. Take a piece of tracing paper fourteen inches long and eight inches wide. This will allow you a one-inch margin all around your pattern. Trace the larger piece of pattern Figure 6 on tracing paper. Place same paper over remaining third of pattern, Figure 6a, matching it to Figure 6, in the manner of a jig-saw puzzle, and complete the tracing. The smaller unit joins the larger unit on the right side, forming a symmetrical pattern which has the three large fruit forms in the center. Do not trace cross-hatching or shading. This is your "master theorem."

Step II. Now take a piece of architect's linen fourteen inches long and eight inches wide and place over your tracing. Trace the whole pattern

FIGURE 6

FIGURE 6A

Motifs to be cut on Master Theorem

FIGURE 6B

PLATE VI, PART I.   BUILT-UP STENCIL

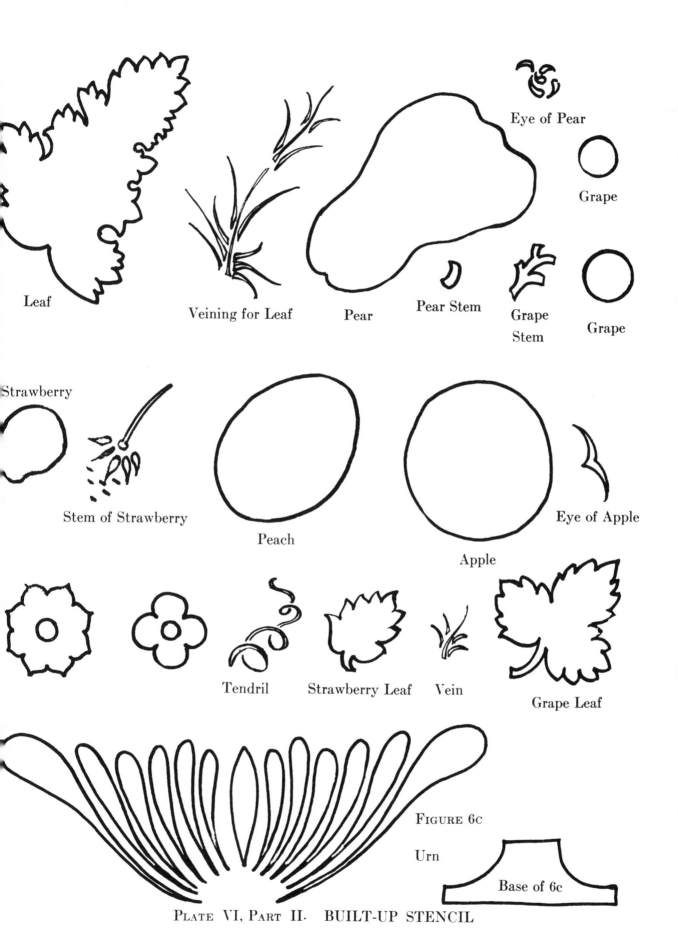

Leaf

Veining for Leaf

Pear

Pear Stem

Eye of Pear

Grape

Grape Stem

Grape

Strawberry

Stem of Strawberry

Peach

Apple

Eye of Apple

Tendril

Strawberry Leaf

Vein

Grape Leaf

FIGURE 6c

Urn

Base of 6c

PLATE VI, PART II.   BUILT-UP STENCIL

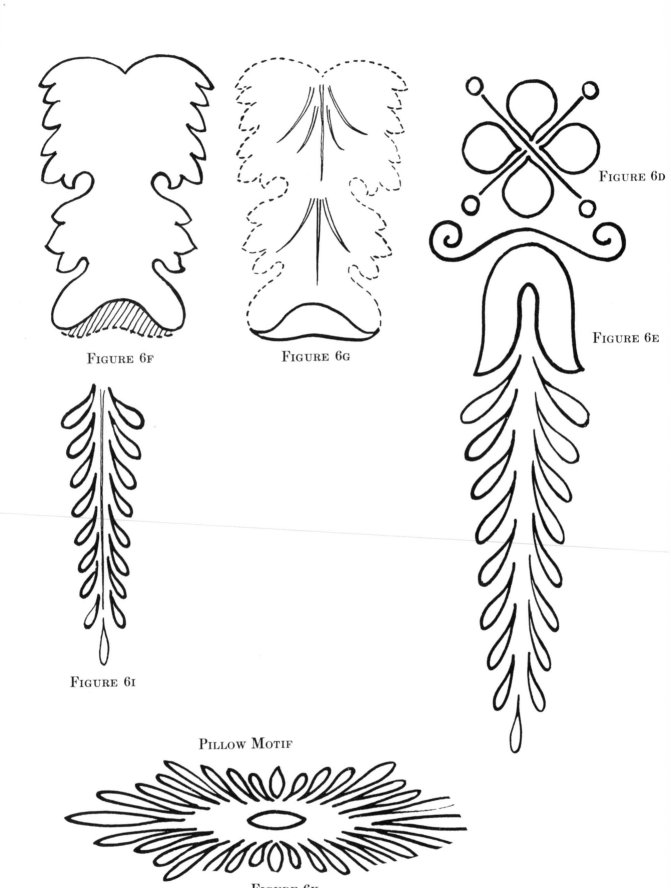

FIGURE 6F

FIGURE 6G

FIGURE 6D

FIGURE 6E

FIGURE 6I

PILLOW MOTIF

FIGURE 6K

PLATE VI, PART III.   BUILT-UP STENCIL

directly on the linen. Cut out all parts that are solid black in Figure 6 and Figure 6a. Use Figure 6b as guide. Figure 6b is the skeleton base on which you will build the complete pattern by adding fruits and leaves one at a time.

Step III. Trace directly on architect's linen the remaining units of the pattern, i.e. the grapes, the strawberry, the pear, the apple, the peach, the tendril, two flower motifs and the large and small leaf. Use a separate piece of linen for each unit, and allow a one-inch margin on each. Cut these out carefully.

Step IV. Before applying the pattern, prepare the chair with two coats of paint. See section on "Preparation of Articles for Decorating" in chapter "General Directions." This chair has a coat of Chinese red overlaid with flat black. The wide slat on which the large design is placed has two coats of flat black with no red undercoat.

Place the chair on its back on a table with the broad slat in a good working position. Varnish the slat, spreading varnish as thinly as possible. Allow it to become almost dry. Have all your materials ready and at hand as the stenciling must be done rapidly when the varnish has reached exactly the right stage to accept the bronze powders.

You will need silver or aluminum powder, brushed brass, and gold leaf or rich gold powder to work out this design. Shadows are put over the stencil later with a thin wash of burnt sienna applied with a brush.

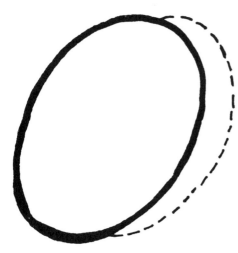

METHOD OF STENCILING

Place skeleton theorem on almost dry varnish and apply silver powder to every cut-out on this master theorem. This will give you your stems, veins, flower centers and tendrils in silver. Carefully remove theorem from chair.

Take pear cut-out and place in position, taking care to have "eye" in proper place at base of pear. Dip finger tip wrapped in velvet in gold leaf powder and apply to pear. Rub in a highlight first with a circular motion, then apply powder from outside edges toward the center, allowing the powder to blur off. This gives an effect of solidity and form to the fruit. Use brushed brass for the apple and apply in the same way. Brushed brass is also used for the peach at the left. Place the stencil in position so that lower edge of peach is on a line with the pear and the left side of peach touches the end of the strawberry stems. After applying the bronze powder, move stencil three-eighths of an inch to the right and one-fourth of an inch upward, and apply powder along the upper rim. This gives the effect of the two mounds of the peach. See small diagram. Black line indicates the position of peach after applying stencil the first time. The broken line indicates the position it should be placed in for the second stenciling. Be careful to brush in only the outer rim of the peach the second time. This will give the effect of shadow between the two sections of the peach.

Place in position large leaf form, laying in carefully over the veining already stenciled on slat. Let upper right end of leaf fade off completely as if leaf were lying under pear. Do small leaves between large fruit and strawberries next, following closely the placing of motifs in drawing of master theorem. Then come both the four-petalled and octagonal flower motifs. These are done in brushed brass. Stencil close to edges of these flowers and let powder blur toward center. This allows silver circle to stand out.

Now you are ready for the strawberries. Place stencil in position and let gold powder fade off to give an effect of strawberry growing out of the small leaves and stem.

In stenciling the grapes, refer to Figure 6 and Figure 6a in book and do *first* the light grapes, *second* the ones shaded in lines and *last* the ones with crosshatching. Let one grape overlap another. Gold leaf powder may be alternated with brushed brass for an interesting effect.

To stencil small leaves at extreme ends of pattern and other background leaves, the tip of the large leaf stencil is used. Place leaf in position and brush the powder on, working from edges toward the center and exerting care to allow the leaf to remain centered over veins which are your guiding lines. In stenciling leaves at top of apple, place light leaf in position first and then do outer edges only of leaf behind it.

Allow pattern to dry completely for at least forty-eight hours. Wash with damp cloth to remove excess gold powder. Complete design by tinting shadow side of fruit with thin wash of burnt sienna using a medium sized sable brush. With a fine pointed quill brush, the stems and veining may be accented in a darker line of burnt sienna.

To complete decoration of chair the following units may be used:

Figure 6d and Figure 6e are used on the front of the seat.

Place Figure 6d at center front and stencil in gold leaf powder. Figure 6e, placed at each side of Figure 6d is done in brushed brass. After stencil is thoroughly dry, wipe off with damp cloth, and add shadow lines with fine pointed quill brush.

If the chair rail at the top back of your chair has a small "pillow" turning in the center, you may use Figure 6k as an alternate stencil for Figure 6d and Figure 6e. This elongated petal motif is a popular one in decorating many of the Hitchcock type chairs and is often found on the front of the seat as well as on the top-rail.

SIDE-POSTS OF CHAIR

Acanthus leaf. Figure 6g and Figure 6h.

Running leaf decoration Figure 6i.

Trace Figure 6f and cut out all except curl at bottom, indicated by shaded lines. Trace Figure 6g and cut veining and curl at bottom of leaf.

Place Figure 6f in position on chair and apply brushed brass powder.

Carefully place Figure 6g over Figure 6f and rub in veining and leaf curl at bottom with gold leaf powder. When dry, accent with fine shadow lines of burnt sienna applied with a hairline quill brush.

Apply Figure 6i, the running leaf pattern, on side posts of chair just under the acanthus leaf, using brushed brass and gold leaf powder. When stenciling is dry, wipe off excess bronze powder with a damp cloth.

Step V. Finishing: Two coats of satin varnish, applied twenty-four hours apart will complete the chair. A smooth glow may be achieved by rubbing final varnish coat, after it has become thoroughly dry, with a soft cloth dipped in crude oil, and a very small amount of rottenstone. Polish with a soft dry cloth.

EXPERIMENTING WITH BUILT-UP STENCILS

For this, you are on your own! We have carefully pointed the way step by step for other designs in the book, but now we are telling you to use your imagination, and build your design alone.

On pages 62 and 63 there are photos of two oblong trays and a round box made by combining the small fruit and leaf units of the Hitchcock chair into a running border decoration.

For the rectangular tray with the grape and leaf border, only the large leaf motif, the two grape motifs and the veining stencil were used. A two-inch border was marked off on the tray. In the middle of each of the four sides, a cluster of grapes was applied with silver powder. The leaves were

BUILT-UP STENCIL FROM UNITS IN PLATE VI, PART 2
For complete directions see "Built-up Stencil," Chapter IV

BUILT-UP STENCIL FROM UNITS IN PLATE VI, PART 2
For complete directions see "Built-up Stencil," Chapter IV

ROUND BOX
Built-up stencil from units in Plate VI, Part 2
Directions on page 61

ANTIQUE TRAY
Owned by Mrs. Langley Keyes, Winchester, Mass.

stencilled in gold, more or less at random. Only the tip of the large leaf was used. Grapes were placed in the corners, and veining in gold was applied to the leaves. If you study the photograph closely you will find that the design is very "hit or miss," the effect of symmetry being achieved by the careful placing of the outer border pattern. For this the running-leaf border Figure 6i is placed end to end on each of the four sides and the tip of the pattern is stencilled in the corners. It is real creative work when you build these patterns without a master theorem.

For the round box, twelve inches in diameter, the strawberry, small leaf, and veinings were used. With a fine striping brush, two circles were painted on the cover; one inside, the other about one and one-half inches apart. This makes a wide border close to the outer edge of the box, within which you build your design. This circular border was then divided into quarters, and at each quarter section a group of three strawberries was stencilled, using brushed brass powder. The tiny leaves or hulls of the strawberries were put on with silver powder, stenciling only a small section of the stem. The single strawberry leaf was applied in clusters of three, using silver powder. These leaf motifs were placed in a close grouping to fill in the rest of the border. For the sides of the box, the running leaf pattern Figure 6i was stenciled in gold-leaf powder, forming a border around the circumference at both top and bottom.

The most amusing design to do is the rectangular tray containing the fruit basket. An extra stencil of the basket must be cut for this (Figure 6c). Then, fill it with fruit and leaves in any manner that suits you. The tendril motif is applied here and there, and the tip of the leaf is tucked back of the fruit as your fancy dictates. (See photograph, page 62). Any border may be used. There are two possibilities in coloring this fruit basket. It is fun to try one of each.

First color scheme: Have at hand small mounds of colored bronze powder in blue, red, green, gold and silver. As you stencil, dip your cloth in blue for the grapes, using silver for high lights, and red and gold for the other fruits. The leaves may be tinted as you stencil, with the green bronze.

Second color scheme: Stencil entire pattern in gold and silver bronze. Allow to dry for at least twenty-four hours and wipe off with a damp cloth. Use alizarin crimson to tint the large fruits and Prussian blue for the grapes. Verdigris thinned with varnish may be used for the leaves and small veins and shadows may be accented with burnt sienna.

Finishing: See section on "Finishing" in chapter "General Directions."

CHAPTER FIVE

SIMPLE BRUSH-STROKE PAINTING

There were two distinct schools of early American brush-stroke painting: that of New England and that of the Pennsylvania Dutch. During the late eighteenth century and first part of the nineteenth, much household furniture was decorated in New England. Flower and vine patterns, primitive figure painting and geometric borders were popular in more or less subdued colors. Ivory scrollwork on brown with small touches of vermilion, several tones of blue on gray or slate color were typical color schemes.

This New England painted furniture is rarely found in antique shops now, and scarcely to be seen outside of museums. However, painted household utensils, canisters, spice sets, syrup jugs, coffeepots, and the like may still be picked up in country antique shops, or resurrected from grandmother's attic. The New England country tin follows a simple decorative pattern with two or three adaptations of standard designs. The colors were vermilion, yellow, olive green or blue green on black or asphaltum backgrounds. A white band was often laid across canisters or coffee pots about one-third of the way down, and on this band a splashing pattern of leaves and cherries or currants was painted. Bright yellow striping and brush stroke borders of great variety added zip and gaiety to the design.

Your grandmother and perhaps even your mother will remember the days when the tin peddlers of New England seemed to appear in the spring with the first pussy willows, their carts laden with plain and fancy tin ware for kitchen and parlor.

The coffin-shaped or oblong octagonal tray was the most popular shape. Most often decorated with a wide band on the floor of the tray, following the shape and close to the sides, their background colors were variations of the love apple, oak leaf, rose leaf, currant, tomato and, above all, the small leaf made with a single brush stroke. Colors were almost never anything but vermilion, green, yellow, black, and white.

The charm of this country painting is its simplicity. There is nothing tight or studied in this naive form of decoration. The sure, swift strokes of the brush which may be seen in every piece of peasant art imported from Europe today pervaded all the early painting in America. There is freedom of movement, joy, and a complete lack of self-consciousness about it. All this is important to remember if you are about to embark on the project of restoring all the painted tin from grandmother's attic. The early brush stroke painting was drawn with the brush — never drawn carefully with a pencil and filled in. You must practise working with a really wet brush until you can control it as well as a pencil, otherwise you will destroy the very effect you are striving for. It is important to have the proper brushes for this work. French quill brushes in three sizes, small, medium and large, should give you a good range and allow you to make almost any brush stroke with one sweep of the wrist.

Folk art reached its highest point in America, not in New England, but in the countryside of Pennsylvania where the Pennsylvania Dutch evolved an interesting and attractive art that is all their own. Of course, the European influence is clearly felt in the forms which are used over and over in their designs. The Tree of Life pattern rising from an urn can be traced back to the Far East. The heart, the rose, the pomegranate, the lily have all been used by early peoples far back into antiquity. But in their color, in their combination of patterns, in their use of symbolism, not only for good luck but as a warder-off of evil spirits, the Pennsylvania Dutch have made a real contribution to our folk art. Even today in riding through rolling Pennsylvania Dutch country you may see freshly painted "hex" signs on barns. The small town museums are owners of many treasures of painted tin, gaily decorated chairs, or dower chests and there is scarcely a home in all the area which does not boast a sgraffito plate or a framed birth certificate dating back a hundred years or more. A complete book could be written on these birth certificates alone. The earliest ones called "fraktur" painting were hand painted and lettered by the schoolmasters who often developed great skill with pen and paints. Mottoes in German reminding the newly born that life is full of tears, and that from the moment the first breath of life is drawn the days are marching inexorably toward the cold grave, are lugubrious in tone but quaintly decorative. Later lithographs were made of these birth certificates and they were colored by hand. Angels, cupids, birds, the Tree of Life, flowers, all these things with symbolism running through the decoration like a golden thread, make the birth certificates interesting to

Figure 8. LARGE SUGAR CANISTER

Figure 7. COFFEE CANISTER
Size eight inches high, five inches diameter
Courtesy of the Society for the Preservation of New England Antiquities

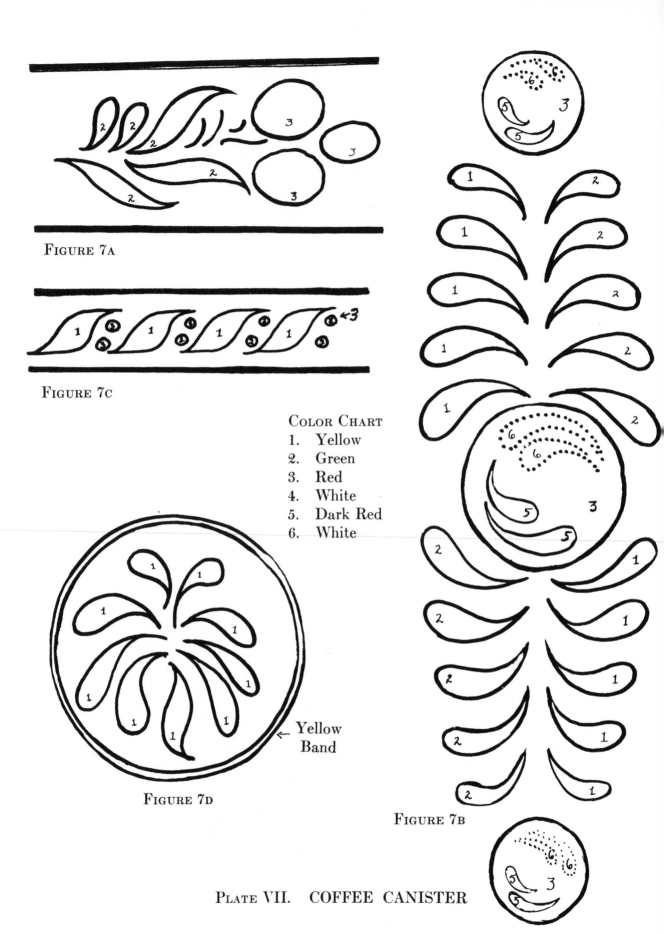

FIGURE 7A

FIGURE 7C

FIGURE 7D

Yellow Band

COLOR CHART
1. Yellow
2. Green
3. Red
4. White
5. Dark Red
6. White

FIGURE 7B

PLATE VII.   COFFEE CANISTER

own even if there is no trace at all of Pennsylvania Dutch in your ancestry.

The dower chests have become the pattern for decorated chests in all parts of the country. Rather more subdued in color than you would expect, with backgrounds often slate gray or brown, the designs are some of the most interesting to be found on any painted furniture. This book uses only one design from a dower chest, the quaint and primitive horseman adapted for a tray in Plate 10, but a volume could be written about the use of the unicorn, the "half-a-king," the urn of flowers and many other motifs which appear in countless variations.

In the decoration of chairs and cabinets, the artisans of Pennsylvania often used the bronze stencil as a base and then painted over it in opaque colors, letting only a small portion of the gilding show. This gives quite a different effect from the use of transparent oils over the bronze stenciling, the method used by the furniture gilders in New York and New England. Philadelphia cabinetmakers followed the New York style of gilding, but in the Pennsylvania country a different technique seems to have developed. Bronze stenciling was used on dark green and dark blue chairs rather than being limited to the black or wood grained backgrounds. Grapes, plums, and apples overpainted in opaque colors make the resulting effect much less formal than that achieved with gold stenciling on black or imitation rosewood.

PLATE VII. COFFEE CANISTER

This simple "love apple" motif is found on so many different pieces of early tin that it has become a standard design. The original design on this coffee tin was almost obliterated, but traces point to the fact that this design or a similar one was on it. In restoring it we applied a pattern sketched from a small syrup jug in the Museum for the Preservation of New England Antiquities, Boston.

DIRECTIONS FOR REPRODUCING

Give the canister two coats of semi-gloss paint in black. Asphaltum makes an attractive background for this pattern and is often used on early tin, but because of peculiar drying qualities, we do not recommend it for beginners.

For the white band which is an inch and a quarter wide, use a white semi-gloss paint, dulled slightly with lampblack. The color should be an "off" white, almost a dirty white. Allow to dry for twenty-four hours.

Read section "Transferring Patterns" in chapter "General Directions."

Trace Figure 7a, which is the design on the white band, and after blacking the reverse side of your tracing paper, apply the motif to the band. The motif is repeated four times.

Trace Figure 7b and apply to center front of can.

The flat leaf border Figure 7c on curved top surface should be transferred next, and finally trace and apply Figure 7d to center of cover of canister.

PAINTING THE DESIGN

Use a mixture of two parts varnish to one part turpentine as a base for painting.

The colors needed are American vermilion, alizarin crimson, raw umber, chrome green, permanent green, chrome yellow, yellow ochre, permalba or Philips white, lampblack.

Make a palette of an old china plate or saucer and squeeze from your Artist's Oil tubes these colors in the following amounts: American vermilion, one-half inch; alizarin crimson, one-fourth inch; chrome yellow medium, one inch; yellow ochre, one-half inch; raw umber, one-half inch; Van Dyke brown, one-fourth inch; chrome green, one inch; permanent green, one-fourth inch.

Use a three-quarter inch quill brush. Paint the buds in the border and the three "love apples" in American vermilion to which you have added small amounts of alizarin crimson and raw umber. The dots in the flat leaf border Figure 7c are also done in vermilion. Parts of design marked 3 are vermilion. For the larger leaves use a sable brush an inch long.

Mix chrome green with permanent green and paint all leaves marked 2. In doing the leaves the best effect is obtained if you use a single brush stroke. Practise it before you start doing your final design and the results will be rewarding. Mix yellow ochre with small amount of chrome yellow medium, allowing enough varnish to make the pigment flow easily and paint the yellow leaves as indicated in the color chart.

The brush stroke motif on the cover Figure 7d may be painted also.

Twenty-four hours later with the same yellow used in the leaves, paint the flat leaf border Figure 7c on curved top surface of the canister. Use the larger sable brush for this border.

STRIPING

Read section on "Striping" in chapter "General Directions."

Using the narrowest striping brush you can find, apply the two stripes in Figure 7c and the stripe in Figure 7d in yellow. The two stripes in Figure 7a should be applied with a slightly wider striping brush, for a quarter-inch stripe of vermilion. A last quarter-inch stripe in yellow is applied around the bottom of the canister.

FINISHING

Read section on "Finishing" in chapter "General Directions." After the design is completely dry, give the canister two coats of satin varnish twenty-four hours apart. After both coats are dry, rub gently with a soft cloth dipped in crude oil and rottenstone.

PLATE VIII. LARGE SUGAR CANISTER

This canister, the original of which is in the museum of the Society for the Preservation of New England Antiquities, is an excellent example of the typical New England decoration on tinware. The free sweeping strokes of the leaves, the almost lyric lines of the pattern and the excellent use of color are each important in making it such a rarely beautiful piece. The combination of American vermilion, dull olive green and bright yellow, set off by an oyster white band, was extremely popular in New England. It was so generally accepted as the proper color scheme for country tinware that it became almost a classic mode. The custom of having one half of the leaves green and the other half yellow, and the technique of outlining veins of dark green leaves in bright yellow was in such general use among apprentice painters that it became a tradition.

DIRECTIONS FOR REPRODUCING

Canisters of all sizes may be bought at hardware stores. This one was six and three-quarters inches high by seven inches in diameter but the design will fit a larger or differently proportioned canister equally well. To enlarge or reduce the design see section "Enlarging and Reducing Patterns" in the chapter "General Directions."

Since most of the canisters available are already enameled in bright colors you will need no priming coat. We have found two coats of black semi-gloss paint a satisfactory base for this type of painting.

After the second coat of black is thoroughly dry, paint the white band one and one-half inches wide, using white semi-gloss paint to which a small amount of lampblack has been added, to gray it a little. The old tinware never had brilliant white banding. It is always a neutral, off white shade. The band in this design comes at the top of the lower half of can, at the groove where the cover fits on.

Transferring the Pattern

When the white band is dry you are ready to place the design. Read section "Transferring the Pattern" in chapter "General Directions." Trace Figure 8a, which is the border, and after blacking the tracing on the reverse side draw the bud and leaf pattern on the white band, repeating the motif all around the canister. On this size canister it should repeat five times.

Next, using the same technique, place Figure 8b on the canister in the center front.

Figure 8c is the border for cover to canister and Figure 8d is the motif for center of cover. The entire cover design is in bright yellow, a combination of chrome yellow medium and yellow ochre.

Painting the Design

Read section on "Technique of Brush Stroke Painting" in chapter "General Directions."

The colors needed are American vermilion, alizarin crimson, yellow ochre, chrome yellow medium, permanent green, chrome green, permalba or Philips white, raw umber.

Brushes: Use a three-quarter inch French quill brush mounted on a stick for all units except the large leaves and the main portion of roses. For these we recommend a rather large sable or camel's hair brush with bristles about an inch long. For the fine scrolls and "flourishes" use a hairline sable brush. For the striping use the thinnest one and one-half inch "sword" striping brush you can buy.

Painting Base: As a mixing medium for your oil pigment use one teaspoon varnish and one-half teaspoon turpentine. Mix more as needed as the varnish has a tendency to thicken as it is subjected to the air.

FIGURE 8B

←YELLOW

←YELLOW

←2

FIGURE 8A

FIGURE 8C

COLOR CHART
1. Vermilion (red)
2. Green
3. Yellow
4. White
5. Dark red

PLATE VIII. LARGE SUGAR CANISTER

FIGURE 8D

Mixing the Paint: An old plate makes an excellent palette. Squeeze out small mounds of paint around edge of the plate, using about an inch of American vermilion, one-quarter inch alizarin, one-half inch each chrome yellow medium and yellow ochre, one-half inch permanent green and one inch chrome green and permalba or Philips white.

Mix vermilion with a small amount of alizarin and a speck of white, thin to painting consistency with your varnish mixture and paint the buds on the border. In the design everything marked 1 should be vermilion.

Next, paint the five roses in the main design. Completely cover the rose with your paint — making no attempt to show the markings of high light and shadow. The shading strokes are added when the first coat of vermilion is bone dry. They should be painted in with a single free hand brush-stroke following the pattern in the book.

For the green leaves combine chrome green with a small amount of permanent green. Add a speck of American vermilion to tone it down a little. Add enough of the varnish and turpentine mixture so that the pigment will flow easily from your brush, and paint leaves in both the border and the main design. Use the large brush for this.

Small dashes of yellow in the main design and a brush-stroke border in yellow on the cover add vivacity to this pattern. The delicate scroll marks are also yellow. Mix yellow ochre with chrome yellow medium, and thin to painting consistency with varnish. Yellow parts of pattern are marked 3. Paint the brush-stroke border on cover of can entirely in yellow. Next, do the medallion in center of cover in yellow. Small touches of yellow appear in the main design. They are marked with the number 3 on the color chart. You will need your finest hairline sable brush for this.

Twenty-four hours later, when the painting is bone dry, the highlights on flowers and buds may be added. Mark the position of the highlights and shadows on the rose with chalk. Mix white with a little varnish and apply brush strokes when white is indicated in pattern. The white parts are numbered 4.

Darken American vermilion by adding a small amount of lampblack and paint in dark brush strokes. The dark parts are numbered 5.

After the pattern has dried, you are ready for the striping. A sixteenth-inch stripe in yellow goes around the cover one-eighth of an inch in from the edge. Two more narrow stripes of yellow are used, one just below the white band and the other three-eighths of an inch up from bottom. At the extreme lower edge of canister, there is a quarter-inch stripe of American vermilion. There are six little touches of American vermilion in the center of the large design. They are indicated by the number 1.

After all painting is thoroughly dry, two coats of satin varnish should be put on the canister allowing ample drying time between coats. A soft sheen is achieved by rubbing the canister with crude oil and rottenstone when varnish has dried.

Figure 9.   ROSE SCROLL TRAY.   Courtesy Mrs. Charles Underwood, Winchester, Mass.

Figure 10.   HORSEMAN TRAY.   Courtesy Philadelphia Museum
Examples of Brush Stroke Painting
For working diagrams see Plates IX and X

CHAPTER SIX

BRUSH-STROKE PAINTING
IN THE MORE ELABORATE MANNER

PLATE IX. ROSE AND SCROLL DESIGN

This brush-stroke design which has been adapted for a circular tray is a much later pattern than the previous ones. The design has been sketched in its original colors from a tin water pitcher, part of a pitcher and basin set owned by Mrs. Charles Underwood of Winchester, Massachusetts. The design is appropriate either as a whole or in part for other painted tin or furniture. You will find that it can be divided with good effect. The two roses with leaves are a nice motif for use on boxes, dresser drawers or chair backs while the scroll lends itself readily to border patterns.

DIRECTIONS FOR REPRODUCING

Brushes: One sable brush about an inch long, one French quill about three-quarters of an inch long.

Paints: Alizarin crimson, permanent green, chrome green, Philips white or permalba, burnt sienna, Van Dyke brown, yellow ochre, raw umber.

A round tray twelve inches in diameter was used for this pattern. It is equally effective, without enlarging any of the motifs on a fourteen or sixteen inch tray. This type of tray is available at most dollar stores. If the tray you select has been enameled, apply two coats of semi-gloss paint twenty-four hours apart. If it is an unfinished tray, be sure that it is free of rust and then give it a priming coat of shellac. Allow to dry at least twenty-four hours. Any background color may be used for this tray. We used black, but a lovely summer tray could be made with this design against an ivory, soft blue or green background.

TRANSFERRING THE DESIGN

Read section "Transferring the Pattern" in chapter "General Directions." When you have traced the motifs from the book and set them on the

COLOR CHART
1. Alizarin (indicated by crosshatching)
2. Creamy pink
3. Creamy tan
4. Green
5. Deep pink

PLATE IX. ROSE AND SCROLL DESIGN

tray in white or dark chalk, depending on your background color, you are ready for the painting.

As a painting base mix one teaspoon varnish with one-half teaspoon turpentine.

To paint the roses, mix alizarin crimson with small amount of white and a dash of raw umber. Paint entire rose in this deep pink. Also do the buds. Allow to become almost dry. When paint does not hold your finger but still feels slightly damp, you are ready to put in the light parts of the rose.

Mix Philips white with a speck of yellow ochre and paint all sections of rose marked 2, allowing paint to blur in with base color of rose as you near the parts indicated by dots in the chart. Allow painting to become bone dry before adding dark shadows indicated on the chart by crosshatching.

For the dark parts use alizarin crimson with a small amount of raw umber. The leaves should be entirely painted with a mixture of chrome green and permanent green, using the quill brush. After they have become bone dry the markings are put in with fine brush strokes in white. You may need a finer brush than the three-quarter inch quill for these markings and for the fine lines in the scroll. A hairline sable brush is good for this delicate work. In the original design the basket, scroll and brush-stroke border were done in a light creamy tan shade, set off with darker brown markings. This color is effective with the pink of the roses on a black or ivory background. If you use a green or blue background the scroll would be interesting done in a darker shade of green or blue, with black or Van Dyke brown markings. Work out a color scheme of your own; it is good fun to experiment.

If you use the tan scroll, mix burnt sienna and Philips white with a speck of raw umber. Paint basket scroll, brush-stroke border and other parts of pattern marked 3. Allow to dry for twenty-four hours.

Use pure Van Dyke brown for markings and shading on scroll and basket. Outline long edge of brush strokes in border, and place a dot of brown at base of other brush strokes.

Finishing

Read section on "Finishing" in chapter "General Directions."

PLATE X. HORSEMAN TRAY

This quaint example of primitive American painting makes a very amusing tray. The design may be adapted for other uses and is especially appropriate for an early American room or a child's room. We sketched the red-coated horseman from a Pennsylvania Dutch chest in the Philadelphia Museum, where he was just one unit in an elaborately painted chest. Although on the chest he was surrounded by geometric borders, scrolls, pomegranates and an urn of tulips, he is quite at home on a circular tray. David Spinner, an early craftsman of Buck's County, Pennsylvania, used this little horseman over and over again on his sgraffito ware plates. The attractive border is actually one of David Spinner's.

DIRECTIONS FOR REPRODUCING

Materials needed: A circular tray either twelve inches in diameter or slightly larger. We have found these in the dollar stores. Since they are already brightly enameled they do not need a priming coat of shellac. Wash the tray. Let it get thoroughly dry before using.

Artist's Oils: American vermilion, yellow ochre, yellow lake, ultramarine blue (or cobalt blue), verdigris (green), permalba. Give the tray two coats flat black allowing twenty-four hours drying time after each coat. Since mistakes are more easily wiped out on a shiny surface than on a dull one, we have found a coat of varnish before starting to transfer the design a help.

TRANSFERRING THE DESIGN

Step I. Trace the design on a good quality tracing paper.

Turn the tracing paper on wrong side and cover lines of pattern, as they show through, with white chalk. (If your tray is a light color use charcoal or black chalk, or even a *very* soft pencil.)

Step II. Cut the tracing to fit floor of tray and place in position with horseman in center, and chalked side facing the tray. Outline in pencil over the tracing so that design in chalk is left on the tray. Do not try to transfer the border until you have completed the center.

Step III. Using varnish, thinned slightly with turpentine as a base, mix a little Philips white or permalba with a dash of American vermilion to make flesh color. Color the head of the horseman flesh color. There is no

FIGURE 10

FIGURE 10A

PLATE X. HORSEMAN TRAY

hair visible except the pigtail which is painted bright yellow, using yellow lake. The pigtail seems to grow right out of a bald pate, which adds to the quaintness of the drawing.

The harness and the outline of the saddle and the stirrup are also done in bright yellow and there is a touch of yellow at the base of the whip in the left hand. The hat and knee breeches are left in black. Simply draw the outline with your brush in white. Use a rather dry brush when outlining hat, whip and legs. Do not forget to put in the highlight on the hat in white. You may outline the horse in white too, and lightly paint the spidery fingers of the left hand. Allow this much of the design to dry. Then paint the horse white. Also paint waistcoat and stockings white. Dry your brush and wipe out a high light on left side of man's leg. Now take a dry, fine-pointed brush and wipe out a few lines in the horse's tail and a shadow on left rear leg to suggest modeling of horse. Your opaque white has covered your line drawing of the horse. Looking at drawing in book, try to replace these lines by drawing on your white horse with a dry brush, until black background shows through. Paint the saddle in ultramarine mixed with very small amount of white. It should be a bright blue.

Paint bottom scroll in verdigris with a dash of white. Cobblestones may be suggested by brush strokes in verdigris.

Allow white paint to dry before attempting to paint red coat.

Paint coat and pigtail in American vermilion. You may need a speck of white in the vermilion to make it bright over the black background. Keep it a good clear red, however.

STRIPING

To prepare for striping give tray one coat of varnish. This makes a slick working surface so that if anything goes wrong with your stripe, you may more easily wipe it out and start again.

The border on this tray is yellow, and consists of an S curve three-eighths of an inch in from the edge, and a one-fourth-inch band on the rim. Use a quill striping brush one and one-half inches long and as narrow as you can buy. To do the S curve, divide circumference of tray into eighths and mark with chalk. Trace the S curve from Figure 10. Whiten the back of tracing with chalk and transfer pattern to tray by drawing pattern in pencil on right side of tracing. This makes a white drawing on tray to guide you in painting.

Figure 11. Pennsylvania Dutch Tray
Courtesy Metropolitan Museum of Art, New York City
For working diagram see Plate 11

Hold brush in thumb and first two fingers by the short quill. Fill with paint and make two or three trial strokes on a piece of practice paper. Then, allowing only tip of brush to contact tray, follow the chalk line and paint in the S curve. Complete eight sections in the same manner.

If you are *very* careful, it is not necessary to let this S curve border become fully dry before striping the outer rim. Stripe a thin line one-fourth of an inch in from rim and then fill in until you complete a one-fourth inch band around edge of tray.

FINISHING

The tray is now ready for finishing. After all painting is thoroughly dry, apply two thin coats of clear varnish, twenty-four hours apart. Read section on "Finishing" in "General Directions"; proceed as indicated.

PLATE XI. PENNSYLVANIA DUTCH OCTAGONAL TRAY

The design for this small Pennsylvania Dutch tray is interesting because it is quite different from the brush-stroke painting designs found on New England tinware. While many of the motifs are the same, the palette is composed of the earth colors so popular with the country painters in Pennsylvania. A striking difference in the color scheme is the use of indigo to make bright blue accents. A warm earthy brown is also used in the Pennsylvania designs. There is also less standardization of units, and more variety in the treatment of the well-known apple, oak-leaf, currant and running-leaf patterns.

The original tray from which this design is taken was painted in 1830 and is in the Metropolitan Museum of Art in New York. The adaptation of the design is made on a tray twelve inches long by nine inches wide.

DIRECTIONS FOR REPRODUCING

Octagonal trays in assorted sizes may be bought in art supply stores and usually come in unfinished tin. They are sometimes called "coffin" trays. Wash and dry the tray, scrubbing thoroughly to remove any protective coating which may have been given the tin to prevent rust.

When tray is bone dry, give it a coat of shellac — any color shellac will do as this is merely a rust preventive. After shellac has dried for at least twenty-four hours, and longer if the weather is damp, give tray two coats of semi-gloss black paint, twenty-four hours apart.

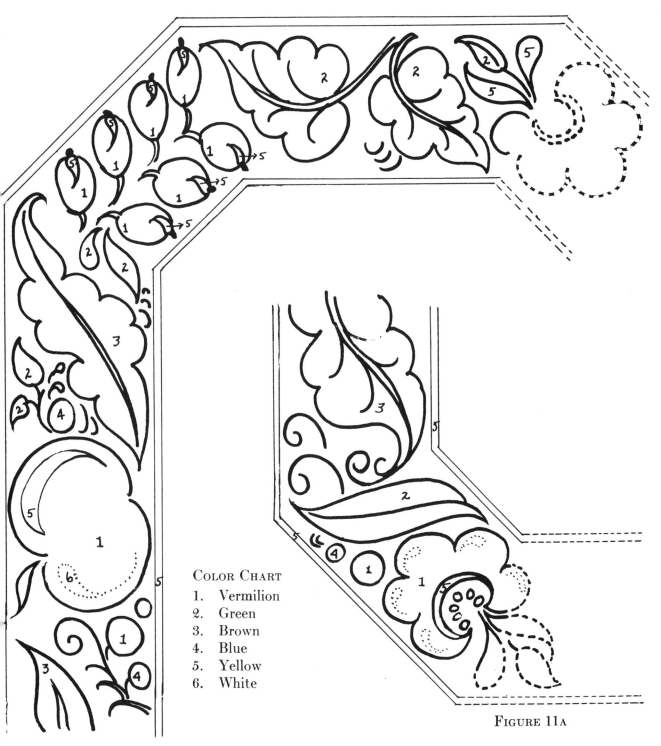

COLOR CHART
1. Vermilion
2. Green
3. Brown
4. Blue
5. Yellow
6. White

FIGURE 11A

FIGURE 11   PLATE XI.   PENNSYLVANIA DUTCH TRAY

To apply white border, measure in two inches from sides of tray on the tray floor and mark a chalk line to indicate the white border. Paint this border in white semi-gloss paint which has been slightly neutralized by adding a small quantity of lampblack. It should be an "oyster" white — a rather "dirty" white when you finish, and the white band should have at least two coats. When the white band is thoroughly dry you are ready to transfer your design. To transfer the design read section on "Transferring the Pattern" in chapter "General Directions."

Colors Needed: American vermilion, chrome yellow medium, yellow ochre, raw umber, permanent green, ultramarine blue, Van Dyke brown, burnt sienna, lampblack, Philips white or permalba.

Brushes: One medium-sized sable brush, one fine pointed French quill brush, one one and one-half-inch long quill striping brush.

Painting the Pattern

In this design colors have been indicated by numbers. Red is 1, green 2, brown 3, etc.

Mix one teaspoon varnish and one-half teaspoon turpentine in an old jar top. This is your "size" with which you will mix your paint.

Squeeze out on a saucer, small quantities of American vermilion, permanent green, yellow ochre, burnt sienna, Philips white, and an even smaller quantity of Van Dyke brown, lampblack, ultramarine blue, chrome yellow medium, and raw umber.

First, mix American vermilion with the varnish and tone down the color with a small amount of raw umber. Paint the tomatoes, flower petals, and currants and all sections marked 1, with vermilion. The green leaves marked with the number 2 are painted next. Use permanent green to which a little white has been added. The brown color for the leaves marked 3 is made by mixing Van Dyke brown and burnt sienna. There are six touches of blue in a small bud indicated by the number 4. It is wise to wait for twenty-four hours before painting the yellow in the pattern, indicated by the number 5. Mix yellow ochre and chrome yellow medium and apply center of flower, one leaf growing from flower and the highlight on one side of tomato. Since the striping is of the same color yellow, it may also be done at this time.

Read section on "Striping" in the chapter "General Directions," and carefully lay the inner stripe on floor of tray one-sixteenth of an inch in width. The outer stripe on floor of tray coming close to side walls is slightly wider, about one-eighth inch. This is applied directly on the white band.

Another fine stripe is applied one-quarter inch down from top on side of tray and the outer rim of the tray has a stripe three-eighths inch in width.

Have a clean cloth ready to wipe off any stripes which waver as you paint them. It often takes several tries to achieve anything resembling good striping.

After all painting has become thoroughly dry, the finishing touches of white and black are added to the design. A high light of white is painted on the tomato, flower, and sides of currants, indicated by the number 6.

It is impossible to indicate by number the black in the pattern, but all veinings, stems and scrolls are painted in lampblack, using the finest quill brush you have.

Each red currant has a dash of yellow at the top and this yellow is tipped with a black dot for accent. The red and blue buds also have a dash of black at the tip, and the stamens of the flower are also in black. Use a free brush-stroke for all this black painting as it is very important in bringing out the beauty of the design.

FINISHING

Read section on "Finishing" in chapter "General Directions."

CHAPTER SEVEN

EIGHTEENTH CENTURY
GOLD AND PAINT DECORATION

PLATE XII. CHIPPENDALE PAINTED TRAY

The Chippendale painted tray shown in the photograph on page 89 is probably the oldest pattern in the book. It is an imported English tray owned by Mrs. Arthur Porter of Norfolk, Virginia. The flower design, where the rose and dahlia are featured, with the morning glory and buds also included, was a popular one with painters of old Japan ware. These elaborately painted black tin trays became very popular in England in the late eighteenth century when the art of "Japanning" was being developed in Sheffield and other places. The baking-on of a hard enamel finish over tin was originally attempted in an effort to imitate the lacquer ware being imported from Japan at this time. Some of the painting on these early trays shows exquisite mastery of the brush. It was whispered in England in 1790 that famous artists were painting trays either for diversion or to eke out income, and examination of the fine handling of paint and pattern in these early trays bears out that statement. Bronze powder was often combined with the oil paint, and on this tray the background is a cloudy bronze, superimposed on the black tray.

DIRECTIONS FOR REPRODUCING

Artist's Oil Paints: Alizarin crimson, chrome yellow medium, yellow ochre, Prussian blue, chrome green, verdigris, Van Dyke brown, burnt sienna, Philips white or permalba.

Bronze Powders: Brushed brass, gold-leaf powder, bronze.

Brushes: A three-quarter inch quill brush, a hairline camel's hair brush.

The Chippendale style tray often called "Gothic," sometimes called "pie-crust," is available in most art supply stores in assorted sizes. The department stores in the larger cities are also stocking these trays in their

Figure 12. Gold Scroll and Flower Tray, Chippendale Pattern

Courtesy Mrs. Arthur Porter, Norfolk, Virginia

For working diagram see Plate 12

Dark Shading

Medium Shading

Light Shading

For colors see text

In transferring pattern trace main outlines
Do not trace shading.

FIGURE 12A

FIGURE 12B

PLATE XII, PART II.   BORDER FOR CHIPPENDALE

FIGURE 12C

art departments, where they may be ordered by mail. The largest size we have found is twenty-five inches by nineteen. If you need a larger tray you will just have to hunt for an antique, or beg some enterprising tinsmith to make one to order.

The antique tray we have reproduced in this book measured seventeen by thirteen inches. The design looks very well, however, without enlargement, on a tray as large as twenty-four by eighteen inches. There would have to be some adapting of the scroll border to fit the larger tray, but it could be managed with imagination and ingenuity. The scroll could also be enlarged by referring to the section "Enlargement of Patterns" in the chapter "General Directions."

Give the tray a coat of shellac as a primer and after this is thoroughly dry, apply two coats of flat black paint twenty-four hours apart. When second coat of flat black is thoroughly dry, give the tray a coat of varnish.

Let this varnish coat reach the "touch" dry stage appropriate for stenciling. Have ready the bronze powder in bronze color. Apply the powder all around the edge of floor of the tray in a cloudy border about an inch and a half in width. Let the cloud fade toward the center and at the base of the curved pie-crust rim of the tray. Allow to dry, and wipe off excess bronze dust with a damp cloth.

Transferring the Pattern

Read section on "Transferring the Pattern" in the chapter "General Directions" and apply the large design in center of the tray.

Figure 12A is the cross-hatching which appears at the center tip on the long side of the tray. Trace and apply this next.

Figure 12B is the scroll for long side of tray. Make two tracings of this. Whiten the reverse side of one, and apply to the tray, placing at left of the cross-hatching. The other tracing should be outlined first on the reverse side. Then whiten the right side of the tracing, and by drawing over your outline on the reverse side, your scroll will fit its position at the right of the cross-hatching. Repeat on other long side.

The longer scroll, Figure 12C, fits across the short ends of the tray without any reversing of the pattern. Make a tracing of this pattern and apply to the tray.

Painting the Design

The gold scroll border of this tray may be reproduced in two different ways.

1. Using a regular gold size or varnish as a medium, mix gold powder with it until it is thick and creamy. Paint the larger forms in the scroll with the quill brush, keeping the finer brush at hand to do the tips of the scroll and cross-hatching. After the entire border has been completed and dried for twenty-four hours shade certain edges of scroll with a fine line of burnt sienna.

2. The second method is the one used on the antique tray we have used as a pattern. It is slightly more complicated but a different effect is obtained. The border is more brilliant and looks a little more professional.

Mix chrome green, permanent green and Philips white in varnish thinned with turpentine. About an ounce should be enough.

Paint the scroll in this bright green. When you have completed a quarter of the border, test your scroll to see if it is almost dry. When it is dry enough so that your finger does not stick but adheres *ever* so slightly, it is ready for the next step. The surface should feel exactly the same as for stenciling. When the painting feels "right," brush over your scroll with a generous application of gold powder, applied with the tip of your finger wrapped in chamois or velvet. If the paint is at exactly the right stage of dryness the gold powder will adhere to the scroll and brush off the surrounding surface. We recommend that you try out this process on a practice tray first. When border is completed, add shadow lines of burnt sienna on right hand lower side of all scrolls. A quarter-inch band of green should go on the outside rim of the tray with gold powder rubbed on. The same technique of underpainting the gold in certain sections of the main design gives an interesting effect. Use the same green mixed for the scroll, adding enough raw umber to dull it somewhat and do parts of the design marked 1. You will need your finest hairline sable brush for tendrils and scrolls. Allow to become "touch" dry and apply gold powder. Rub gold only in center of leaves, leaving edges and tips green. The tendrils and scrolls are entirely covered with gold.

The flowers should be painted next. For the rose, mix Philips white with a little yellow ochre. The paint should be an ivory color, and held almost transparent by using more varnish than pigment. The rose should be painted solidly in this color. The asters and buds marked 3 should also be painted this transparent ivory.

For the morning glory use Prussian blue with a speck of Philips white, painting the entire blossom and buds above it in this color. Add more white to the Prussian blue and paint the petals of the asters marked 4, in the lower left and right corners of the design. Do not paint the center or stamen section of the asters blue. The petals of the dahlia, the large flower at the right of the rose, should be painted in alizarin crimson darkened with raw umber.

A small amount of white should be added to make the color visible against the black background. Stamens for all the flowers are painted in chrome yellow mixed with yellow ochre and white. Allow paint to dry. The next day, now that the entire pattern has been blocked in and has become thoroughly dry, the excess bronze powder may be wiped off with a damp cloth.

You are now ready to add shading and overpainting to the flowers.

Take a small amount of Philips white dulled with a speck of yellow ochre and paint part of morning glory marked 5. Using your finest brush, make a fine white line around outer rim of morning glory. Add highlights in this same color to section of morning glory buds marked 6.

With a single brush stroke, tip the edges of the blue aster petals with this same color.

For the highlights on the petals of the larger daisies and buds at the top right and left of the design, use a mixture of Philips white and yellow ochre, making it less transparent than for your first application of color.

Add a small amount of alizarin crimson to the yellow ochre and white, and paint the central section of the rose, shown in the chart with dots. Outline the outer petals in this color, which should be more ivory than pink. Allow to dry.

The next day the painting of the shading on the flowers may be completed.

Use alizarin crimson with a speck of raw umber in varnish to add the deep shadows on the rose. Keep the paint transparent by using plenty of varnish. All parts of rose shown by cross-hatching should be in this color.

With a single brush stroke, suggest a shadow on the right side of each bud with alizarin, dulled with raw umber. Wash in a round, solid circle of alizarin in the center of the asters, letting it extend around the base of the petals. For the shading on the petals of the dahlia, add yellow ochre and white to alizarin and paint the left half of each petal. Outline right side of petal in a very dark tone of alizarin.

For the veining in the leaves, use burnt sienna lightened with a little Philips white.

A final retouching of the stamens of the flowers with yellow ochre mixed with white completes the painting. Three or four small stamens should be added to the dark central section of the rose, and two or three painted in the center of the daisies. The round circle of stamens in the dahlia may be retouched with touches of burnt sienna to give depth.

FINISHING

Read section "Finishing" in chapter "General Directions" and proceed accordingly.

CONCLUSION

We have tried to be exact in our directions and we hope you have had fun experimenting. Certain things have been difficult to explain without colored diagrams. Certain other things such as striping and shading a rose have made us pause, as we fancied you attempting them for the first time.

Our wish is that you have liked your excursion into the art of decorating well enough to spend many pleasant hours wielding a paint brush or a finger dipped in bronze dust.